BEGINNER'S GUIDE TO
Brass Rubbing

BEGINNER'S GUIDE TO

Brass Rubbing

RICHARD J. BUSBY

PELHAM BOOKS

First published in Great Britain by
PELHAM BOOKS LTD
26 Bloomsbury Street
London, W.C.1
1969

7207 0244 5

Set and printed in Great Britain by
Tonbridge Printers Ltd, Peach Hall Works, Tonbridge, Kent,
in Bell eleven on fourteen point, and bound by
James Burn at Esher, Surrey

To

JANET AND DAVID

CONTENTS

INTRODUCTION   11

1 HISTORICAL INTRODUCTION TO BRASSES AND BRASS
  RUBBING   13

Origin of Brasses. Composition of Brass.
Manufacture of Brass. Engraving. Design.
Cost. Distribution. Destruction. Palimpsest
Brasses. History of Brass Rubbing. References

2 THE TECHNIQUE OF BRASS RUBBING:
  (1) TRADITIONAL METHODS   31

Materials Required. Obtaining Permission.
Making a Rubbing. Note-taking. Rubbing
Mural Brasses, Problems of. Care of Brasses
When Making Rubbings

3 THE TECHNIQUE OF BRASS RUBBING:
  (2) ALTERNATIVE METHODS   47

New Materials, Crayons, Colours. Reverse
Rubbings. Dabbings. 'Rubbings' on Aluminium
Foil

4 THE DISPLAY AND STORAGE OF RUBBINGS   55

Display in the Home. Mounting Rubbings.
Photographing Rubbings. Screen Printing from
Rubbings. Public Exhibitions of Rubbings.

Facsimiles of Brasses. Storage of Rubbings. Cataloguing a Collection. Indexing a Collection

5 HOW TO FIND OUT ABOUT BRASSES   76

Location Lists: British Isles. Continental Brasses. General Books on Brasses, British Isles. Books, Periodical Articles, about the Brasses in Individual Counties of the British Isles. Mainland Europe. Costume. Armour. National Collections of Brass Rubbings in the U.K. The Monumental Brass Society.

APPENDIX   106

INDEX   121

ILLUSTRATIONS

between pages 24 & 25

1 Sir John Peryent and wife Joan, 1415. Digswell, Herts.

2 Edward Humberstone and wife Annas, 1583. Walkern, Herts.

3 Reverse side of brass in Plate 2

4 Abbot Thomas de la Mare, c. 1370. St Albans Abbey, Herts.

5 The Author brass rubbing at Digswell Church, Herts.   *facing page* 32

6 Sir William Roberts and two wives, 1508. Little Braxted, Essex   33

7 Elizabeth Parker, 1602. Radwell, Herts.   48

8 Sir John Peryent (jnr), 1442. Digswell, Herts.   49

9 Rev. Richard Folcard, 1451. Pakefield, Suffolk (reverse rubbing)   64

10 Knight, c. 1500. Rubbing on aluminium foil   65

11 Sir John Poyle and wife Elizabeth, 1424. Hampton-Poyle, Oxfordshire. Rubbing on aluminium foil   80

12 Sir John Seyntmour and wife Elizabeth, 1485. Beckington, Somerset (screen print from brass rubbing)   81

13 Facsimile of brass in Plate 8 by Laurent
   Designs Ltd   96

14 Roger Thornton and wife, 1429. All Saints',
   Newcastle-on-Tyne   97

15 Indent of brass of Bishop Beaumont (ob. 1333).
   Durham Cathedral   112

16 (a) St Alban. (b) King Offa. (Figures from
   brass of Abbot Thomas de la Mare, c. 1370, St
   Albans Abbey, Herts.)   113

INTRODUCTION

A great many books and articles have been written about church brasses in the last one hundred years, but very few of these deal with brass rubbing in any detail.

In the following pages will be found not only a detailed description of brass rubbing using the traditional medium – black heel-ball on white paper – but short notes on adaptations of this method using new materials and techniques. The object of this is to inspire not only the beginner, but also the more practised enthusiast, to take a more active interest in his collection. Nearly all of the ideas listed are capable of modification or extension, and no attempt at comprehensiveness is intended in these sections. I would, indeed be glad to hear from any readers who know of alternative methods of making or using rubbings, especially for decorative purposes.

The inclusion of a lengthy and detailed bibliography on the literature of brasses – in which all the major English language works of any importance are listed – should help those so inclined to find their way about the subject. For those more interested in their local area only, the county or regional lists of books and periodical articles should act as a useful guide. The main problem with many of the items noted will be the purely physical one of seeing or obtaining copies in Public Reference or lending libraries; unfortunately this is especially the case with the Transactions of the Monumental Brass Society, of which few libraries hold complete sets.

For help in the compilation of this book I must thank especially the Society of Antiquaries, the Hertfordshire County Library, the Aluminium Federation, Laurent Designs Ltd, the East Herts. Archaeological Society, Mr Peter Catterick, the Monumental Brass Society, Miss J. Crallan (for much help with the details of screen printing from brass rubbings), Mrs G. Gillard (for the invaluable task of typing the manuscript) and last, but not least, my wife Janet who has had to suffer more than her fair share of baby-minding and household chores whilst this book was being written.

R.J.B.
WELWYN GARDEN CITY

1

Historical Introduction to Brasses and Brass Rubbing

Origin of brasses. Composition of brass. Manufacture of brass.
Engraving. Design. Cost. Distribution. Destruction. Palimpsest
brasses. History of brass rubbing. References.

Origin of brasses

It is over 750 years since the first brass was laid down
in an English church. Very simple in design, it consisted of
a large cross springing from a quadrangular base, and was
in memory of Simon de Beauchamp, founder of Newnham
Priory, near Bedford (ob. 1208). The slab was in St Paul's
Church, Bedford, but unfortunately cannot now be
identified with any certainty.

Since that date, and for the next 550 years, a long
and varied succession of brasses were laid down in
Great Britain and Western Europe. It is estimated that
today about 4,000 figure brasses (plus about 3,000
memorials consisting of inscriptions only) still survive
in the British Isles. On the continent about 400 examples
have been recorded, but these totals are thought to
represent only about one quarter of those originally
laid down.

It is now generally accepted that brasses and brass
engraving had their beginnings on the Continent of
Europe, probably in the Low Countries or Germany, in

13

the late twelfth century. The earliest known engraved brass of any description is an inscription at Regensburg in Southern Germany, dated 1189. The exact origin of brasses is obscure; most of the early writers on the subject draw comparisons between brasses, Limoges enamels and incised slabs. Many also point out the high cost of stone monuments, and the inconvenience caused by early stone effigies, carved in low relief and set into the floor of the church; as these became more numerous they began to interfere with the free passage of processions and passersby. In addition to these facts, it is painfully evident how susceptible stone monuments were to the knives of doodlers, initial carvers and souvenir hunters.

An alternative, and more practical form of stone memorial was the incised slab. These were in use long before brasses, but the great similarity between the two would seem to indicate a common source. It is known with some certainty, that masons also worked in other media, and the methods and tools used for engraving both metal and stone are very similar. The English mason Henry Yevele (ob. 1400) refers in his will to his tools for 'graving in platte'.

Incised slabs had, however, one great disadvantage over their three dimensional counterparts—their natural tendency to wear away when placed in busy thoroughfares. In common with figures in the round, they were also very costly to transport to areas where natural stone was not in abundance e.g. East Anglia; the Home Counties; the Netherlands. On the continent many of the same problems arose, and it was not altogether unnatural that makers of church monuments should search around for a more durable, permanent and cheaper medium in which to work.

14

Abundant natural resources meant that by the end of the twelfth century the metal industry was already well established in Northern Europe. Cast metal tombs were already beginning to appear, and brass, or as it was more commonly known, laton (or latten) was in extensive use for both domestic and ecclesiastical vessels, ornaments, etc. As laton was usually cast in sheet form and was then beaten flat, the idea of using the flat plates and engraving them, was almost a natural outcome of incised work in stone, and normal metal work decoration i.e. gold, silver and copper engraving. The reverse of a palimpsest brass at Great Berkhamsted, Herts. bears a very lightly engraved portion of the brass and inscription in memory of Thomas Humfre of London, Goldsmith (*c.* 1500); the delicacy of the engraving would seem to indicate that it was done by someone like a goldsmith, more used to working in precious metals than in laton.

One other important fact which helped, not only to establish, but to retain, the monopoly of brass manufacture in Northern Europe, were the vast deposits of copper (the largest single constituent in laton) and calamite (or zinc) ore which is essential during the smelting of the metal. Calamite was not discovered in England until 1566, when it was found in Somerset. This is not to say that from the earliest appearance of brasses no engraving was done in England; mainland Europe simply produced all the brass itself and exported it in sheets to Britain. Schools of engraving were established very quickly in both places, but as will be seen later, their final designs were often very different. When brass was finally manufactured in England in Elizabeth I's reign, it was of inferior quality, made of much thinner metal and came too late to save what was fast becoming a dying art.

What is a brass and how was it made?

Technically, the word 'brass' applies more to the material than to the memorial itself, since any alloy such as this was given a similar general designation. To our medieval ancestors the terms church brasses, sepulchral brasses, memorial brasses or monumental brasses, as they have been variously called, would have meant little. They were more commonly referred to in contemporary terminology as 'latten' or 'laton' plates, the word 'brass' not being in general use until about the beginning of the sixteenth century. Other documents (e.g. contracts, wills) refer to them as 'cullen plates', a corruption of the name Cologne in Germany, one of the many centres of the brass industry. A contract dated 1st March, 1536, between Sir William Sandys and a Dutch tomb maker Arnout Hermanszoen, refers to the metal as *cuivre blancq* (white copper).

The metal itself is basically an alloy consisting mainly of copper and zinc, with small quantities of lead and tin. Tables showing details of analysis of eight early brasses are reproduced in Volume 2 of Leslie Aitcheson's invaluable book *A History of metals* p. 324 (Macdonald & Evans. 2 vols. 1960). The metal having been cast in shallow moulds, it was then hammered into plates averaging about three feet by two and a half feet in size, and of varying thickness. The marks of the hammer made during this 'process of battery' can be clearly seen on the reverse of many brasses. Examination of larger brasses will soon reveal that they were composed of, or engraved from, several sheets of brass joined together, e.g. any of the large Flemish brasses show this well.

Workers in sheet brass, or 'yellow metal', were called 'lattoners', and while they often made other items besides brasses, it would seem that the term was one more usually reserved for makers of church brasses. L. F. Salzman in his famous book *Building in England down to 1540* (Oxford, Clarendon P. 1952 repr. 1967) quotes the case of one William Latoner who sold six weather vanes of laton to Sheppey Castle in 1365 (p. 236).

The method of engraving the brass was not dissimilar to that of stone. A cold chisel, a mallet and a burin were the principle tools, the design presumably being scratched, painted or chalked on to the plates first; templates may even have been employed when mass production of brasses was at its height in the early sixteenth century e.g. for groups of children. It is known that these were employed for the designs of stone and wooden monuments. The 'false moulds' or templates were made of wood or parchment and had the pattern engraved on them. It does not seem unlikely that similar media were used for the designs of brasses and may well have been sent to the Low Countries and elsewhere when an order was placed.

The engravers themselves have largely remained anonymous as very few brasses are signed. One often quoted early example is that of Sir John Creke and his wife (*c.* 1325), Westley Waterless, Cambs., which bears the mark of an N, a star and a mallet, believed to be the seal or mark of Walter the Mason; the mark can be seen below the feet of Lady Creke. On the continent the famous families of Vischer of Nürnberg and Hilliger of Freiberg are known to have worked in brass as well as other metals. Readers requiring further information on this subject are referred to Malcolm Norris' book *Brass Rubbing* (pp 71–79 especially).

It will not take the beginner long to notice that many brasses exhibited marked similarities in style, and it has long been recognised that certain centres or schools of engraving existed both in England and abroad. These were not necessarily the same places as where the brass itself was manufactured. In England, known centres were in or near Norwich, Ipswich, London, Cambridge, Bristol, Coventry and York. On the continent important centres existed in or around Cologne, Hamburg, Nürnberg, Meissen, Lübeck, Zeitz, Ghent, Liége, Paris and Cracow.

Once the brass had been engraved, the stone slab had to be dressed, a matrix cut to receive the plates, and rivet holes bored in it for fixing down the pieces. Before the final fixing took place, the back of the brass was coated with mastic (usually bitumen) to stop chemical reaction taking place between the metal and the bare stone, and to reduce the risk of moisture forming underneath. Once positioned in its matrix the plate was finally secured with brass rivets set in lead plugs let into the stone (on the modern raw plug principle); the rivet heads were then flattened out and rubbed smooth so that they lay flush with the surface of the surrounding metal.

One will sometimes see brasses to which coloured enamels have been added, though in many cases only very small traces of this remain. The most famous example is the shield carried by Sir John D'Abernon (1277) which still retains its original blue colouring. The brass of Sir John Say and his wife (1473) at Broxbourne Church, Herts., bears many traces of red enamel. It was the presence of colouring on brasses which presumably caused early writers like Haines (*cf. bibliog. p.* 80) to connect the origin of brasses with Limoges enamels.

Finally, a few points must be made about the actual design of the brasses themselves. Malcolm Norris has much to say on this point both in his book (*op. cit.*) and in his excellent paper on *Schools of Brasses in Germany* (see end of chapter for details), and readers are referred to these for fuller information. In very general terms it can be said that continental brasses were mostly engraved on plates fitted together to form one solid area of brass, the background being filled in with diaper worker, allegorical designs, etc. e.g. Abbot Thomas de la Mare (*c.* 1370) St Albans Abbey, Herts; Bishop Ludolph and Henry Von Bülow (1347), Schwerin, E. Germany.

Local variations in both design and execution are clearly visible, and many of the brasses show the figure as if still alive rather than in a recumbent position e.g. Jacob Schelewaerts (1483), Bruges, Belgium. Mr Norris shows an example on p. 69 of his book of how the figures in the side shafts of the canopy on Cardinal Frederick Casmiri's brass at Cracow, Poland (1510) were copied from an earlier woodcut by Dürer. Nearly all the continental brasses are very large.

In contrast to the above, the English brasses were generally smaller with the background cut away, the figure(s), canopy, inscription(s), shields, scrolls, all being engraved as individual pieces. This was done for reasons of economy as much as any other, and as evidence of this a small Flemish brass of a priest (*c.* 1365) at North Mimms, Herts. has had the background and surrounding border and inscription cut away to make it conform to the English pattern. The largest brass ever recorded does happen to be an English example and the matrix (with figure restored) can be seen in Durham Cathedral. This was in memory of Bishop Ludvic Von Beaumont (ob. 1333) and measured over 15 feet high by nearly 10 feet wide. In contrast, the figure of an anonymous civilian (*c.* 1520) at Chinnor, Oxfordshire, is only 7¼ inches high.

Who used brasses and how much did they cost?

As indicated above, brasses could be made in any size, so it is not surprising that by the early sixteenth century they were being used by all but the very poorest classes of the population. The classification in Chapter 4, page 71, will give a good idea of the various types that will be encountered. The size and magnificence of a brass was, like most other things, largely dependent on how much the purchaser was prepared to pay. All too little is known at present about the cost of brasses because few records have survived, and to try and equate the few examples known with modern values is almost impossible. The ledger of a Scottish trader in Holland, Andrew Halyburton, shows that in 1494 the exchange rate was $2\frac{1}{2}$ English to 6 Flemish groats (i.e. £1 sterling equalling £2 8s. 0d. Flemish). For the brass of William Catesby and his wife (1505) at Ashby St Legers, Northants, showing the figures in heraldic dress under a double canopy, £6 13s. 4d. was bequeathed in Catesby's will.

A much better, and often quoted example, is that of the brass of Dr Duncan Liddel (ob. 1613) in St Nicholas Church, Aberdeen. This is a large brass plate some $5\frac{1}{2}$ by 3 feet, engraved at Antwerp, showing the Doctor seated at a table in his study. Contemporary Burgh records show that the total cost of this memorial was £121 15s. 6d.

This total was made up approximately as follows:

Material (219 lb. of metal)	£31 0s. 6d.
Engraving	£53 0s. 0d.
Transport; import duty etc; travelling expenses on behalf of executors for three return trips to Antwerp	

(by their agent (?))   £37 15s. 0d.
                                         _____

                                          £121 15s. 6d.
                                         _____

For the laying of the stone and fixing of the brass
Alexander Wyisman charged an additional £10 Scottish.

Distribution of brasses

East Anglia and the Home Counties are far above the
other counties in terms of numbers of brasses, Kent, Essex,
Norfolk and Suffolk all have over two hundred figure
brasses. In proportion to their size counties like Oxfordshire, Bedfordshire, Buckinghamshire and Hertfordshire
are rich in brasses. The Northern and Midland counties
are mostly small in numbers; Cumberland, Northumberland, Westmorland and Durham containing only some
twenty-five figure brasses between them (those with
inscriptions only are more numerous). Scotland, Wales
and Ireland contain very few examples, and on the continent, of the four hundred or so recorded to date, most
are in Germany, Poland and Belgium; a few can be seen in
the Scandinavian countries, Spain, Portugal and Italy.
Those remaining represent, as in the British Isles, only a
very small proportion of the original total, Holland and
France, for example, having lost almost all their brasses.
All enthusiasts travelling abroad are asked to look out for
hitherto unrecorded examples and report them to the
Monumental Brass Society.

The destruction of brasses

A few notes are necessary here to explain the fate of so
many brasses. The reasons can basically be divided into
six categories:

(1) Destruction resulting from religious and political upheavals e.g. the Dissolution of the Monasteries in England; Calvinist wars in Northern Europe; French Revolution; Cromwell's Protectorship of England; two World Wars.

(2) Deliberate or ignorant destruction for financial reasons e.g. selling the brass for the value of the metal.

(3) Superstition – allied to (i) above, e.g. all representation of the Holy Trinity were a target for religious zealots like the anti-Papists, who stripped most churches of 'all superstitious images and inscriptions'.

(4) The 'Churchwarden' period in the late eighteenth and early nineteenth century when churches not only fell into decay, but many of the brasses were deliberately sold.

(5) The Gothic revival of Victorian England when extensive 'beautification' and restoration of churches and Cathedrals took place, often resulting in a clean sweep of all the brasses.

(6) Theft.

A few examples should suffice to illustrate the above points:

(a) *Lincoln Cathedral, 1655.* John Evelyn records in his diary for 19th August, 1655:

'The souldiers had lately knocked off most of the brasses from the gravestones, so as few inscriptions were left; they told us that these men went in with axes and hammers, and shut themselves in, till they had rent and torne off some barge-loads of metall, not sparing even the monuments of the dead, so hellish an avarice possessed them. . .'

(b) *Suffolk, 1643–44.* During his office as 'reformer' of parish churches in East Anglia, William Dowsing boasts in his journal of having destroyed 192 brasses in 52 churches. On 6th January, 1644, he received 11s. 8d. for 40 lb. of brass.

(c) *St Margaret's Westminster, 1644.* For 29 lb. of fine brass and 96 lb. of coarse brass 'taken off sundrie tombe-stones in the church' £1. 13s. 6d. was paid to the Church-wardens.

(d) *Shrewsbury (St Alkmund's), Salop., 1794.* Brasses sold by order of the Churchwardens to a neighbouring brazier.

(e) *Meopham, Kent. (early eighteenth century).* Because of shortage of metal when recasting the bells 'some persons tore off all the brass inscriptions from stones in the church . . . and threw them into the melting pot . . .'

(f) *Hook Norton, Oxfordshire (mid nineteenth century).* An inscription dated 1497 sent by a local farmer (also a Churchwarden) to the blacksmith for the latter to repair his plough with, but it proved to be of no use as it was the wrong metal for the job.

(g) *Playford, Suffolk. (1840's).* It was reported to the Committee of the British Archaeological Association in March, 1844 that the brass of Sir John Felbrigg (1400) had been torn up and the pieces placed in the church chest. Although subsequently refixed, many parts were lost in the process. (*Archaeol. Journal,* Vol. I (1844) p. 70).

Other brasses have at various times been found doing duty as parts of a weather vane (York Minster); a sundial; a fire-back (e.g. Kelshall, Herts., 1527); and door scraper (e.g. Royston, Herts., c. 1500). At Aldenham, Herts in the nineteenth century it was reported that many of the slabs from the church, complete with brasses, were used by a local baker to line his ovens; the uniqueness of the patterns on his loaves led to a great increase in his sales!

These are examples of past abuses, but even as I was writing this book it was reported in the April, 1968 *Newsletter of the Monumental Brass Society* that the brasses at Great Amwell, Herts. (*c.* 1440) and Packington, Leics., (*c.* 1450) had been stolen from their churches.

Palimpsest brasses

Distribution and theft of brasses leads me to make special mention of a unique class of brasses – namely palimpsests. Although this is a blanket term covering three distinct types, the word itself comes from the Greek and literally translated means 'used again'. In its original context it referred to manuscripts, but in the case of brasses the most common types of palimpsest encountered are those where pieces of brass have been turned over and re-engraved on the reverse of the original. Many of the original brasses were stolen from the continent, especially during the mid and late sixteenth century; others came from local English sources, e.g. the Monasteries, following the Dissolution. Good examples of the above type are at Harrow, Middlesex (1579); Walkern, Herts. (1583) – new ones are discovered almost every year, and many of these are recorded in the Transactions of the Monumental Brass Society. In the churches themselves some will be found framed, hinged, mounted or electro-typed so that both sides can be readily inspected.

The other classes of palimpsest which will be met with are as follows:

(1) Appropriated brasses – usually instanced by a later inscription and/or shields being added to an earlier brass e.g. Bromham, Bedfordshire (1435 to 1532). In other cases a stolen figure of earlier date was added to a new figure and/or inscription (e.g. Digswell, Herts. figures

Plate 1.
Sir John Peryent
and wife Joan. 1415
Digswell,
Hertfordshire. Two
fine, life-size figures
engraved when
English brasses were
at their best.
Note Lady Joan's
magnificent plaited
head-dress and the
unusual animals at the
feet of the two figures
– a leopard and a
hedgehog. Rubbing
brasses of this size
requires both patience
and skill in order to
obtain this result.
From a rubbing
by the author

Plate 2. *Obverse*. Edward Humberstone and wife Annas 1583.
Walkern Hertfordshire. When this apparently ordinary
civilian brass was taken up some seventy years ago it was
found to be palimpsest. As the illustration opposite shows, it
is composed of eleven pieces cut from various earlier Flemish
brasses. (*See Chapter 1.*) Photo: Henry W. Gray. Rubbing
by the author

Plate 3. *Reverse* of palimpsest brass shown in Plate 2 opposite. The pieces making up the reverse of this brass date from between *c.* 1400 and *c.* 1500. The piece from which the heraldic achievement above the figures has been cut bears the date 1474 on the reverse. The two plates on which the children are engraved fit together to form part of a shield bearing the Arms of Gryse. Other pieces of the same Flemish brass have been found at Marsworth, Bucks and other churches in the Home Counties. (*See Chapter 1.*) Photo: Henry W. Gray. Rubbing by the author

Plate 4.
Abbot Thomas de
la Mare. *c.* 1370. St Albans
Abbey, Hertfordshire. The
finest Flemish ecclesiastical
brass in England, measuring
9 ft 3 in. by 4 ft 4 in. It is
said that this brass was
turned on its face during
Oliver Cromwell's
Protectorship to save it
from destruction by his
'reformers'. Because of the
great reduction in size
necessary to photograph
this rubbing much of the
fine detail has been lost.
(*See Chapter 1.*) Photo:
Peter Goldsmith. Rubbing
by the author

c. 1520; inscription, 1557). At Edlesborough, Bucks. (1540) an earlier stone has been appropriated for later figures, and in one rare instance at Okeover, Staffs., the existing figures of 1447 have been adapted to suit the fashions of 1538.

(2) Wasters – were brasses which, because of some fault in the first design, were turned over and re-engraved correctly e.g. Walton-on-Thames, Surrey. (1587). Another type of waster is one on which doodles or practice designs appear on the reverse of the brass, e.g. Colby, Norfolk (1508); these were presumably done by apprentices in the workshop.

Indents of brasses

One final point allied to the destruction of brasses, is the recording of indents (or matrices) of lost brasses. Little attention has been given to these in the past, but they are, in their way, almost more important than the brasses which survive, since they are the only remaining evidence of the existence of the memorial. Their recording and preservation is one of the main objects of the Monumental Brass Society, who are hoping to set up teams in each county and abroad to record all existing examples. Far too many have been destroyed already as being of no value or interest, and others will no doubt follow as floors are relaid – this makes the Society's task even more urgent. Notes on making 'dabbings' of indents as a means of recording them are given in a later chapter.

Early brass rubbings

The exact origin of brass rubbing is obscure, but a painting dated 1633 in the Baltimore Museum of Art entitled 'Interior of the Great Church at Delft' shows a group of children taking stone rubbings. The antiquary Richard Gough was one of the first English writers to study brasses in any great detail, and when collecting material for his famous book *The Sepulchral Monuments of Great Britain* . . . (pub. in 1786–96) he had impressions made of several brasses. Three pages of these are reproduced in his book, all from Leatheringham, Suffolk, and because of the way they were made, are all in reverse. These impressions or 'blackings' were first made by friends and contemporaries of Gough's – Craven Ord (1756–1832) and Sir John Cullum (1733–1785), who began work in about 1780. Their combined efforts are in the British Museum (see p. 103 for details).

Their method of operation would horrify modern church authorities, and because of its uniqueness I will describe it briefly below. Having arrived at the church on horseback with all their materials, they covered the brass with printing ink, cleaned off the surplus ink and laid thick, previously damped, paper over the surface. Then, using flannels, and some means of pressure that they could best devise, they rolled these over the paper so that the ink which had filled the incised lines of the brass was transferred to the paper, leaving on it an impression in reverse. Where uneven pressure had given a poor image, the faults were made good with pen and ink or a brush; on other occasions a very light impression was taken which was later, with considerable labour, inked in with a pen and/or brush. Nearly one hundred of these impressions survive thanks to the generosity of Mr Francis Douce who bequeathed them to the nation in 1834.

Because of the inconvenience of the above method, other experiments were tried. One was using a lead plummet, but this being so hard, it tended to tear the paper easily;

lumps of black lead (pencil lead) were also tried with some success, a refinement on this being the use of the large black-leaded carpenter's pencil. The latter was fixed afterwards, to prevent smudging, with a mixture of milk and beer! Other enthusiasts experimented with soft black leather rubbers made of waste pieces which had become impregnated with the dubbing or black compound with which the skins were first dressed. By the late 1830s, however, the firm of Messrs Ullathorne of Long Acre, London, had perfected a heel-ball highly suitable for brass rubbing, very similar in composition to that in use today. Made principally of bees-wax, tallow and lamp black, it was available both in stick and cake form (in pieces about three inches in diameter). They also supplied a waxy compound of a yellow colour to resemble the original brass. All were available in various degrees of hardness to suit the particular condition of the brass or the outside temperature (in hot weather a harder quality is more useful).

Other manufacturers followed suit, and one, Mr H. S. Richardson of Greenwich, devised a metallic rubber to be used with dark coloured or black paper; this resembled very closely the original brass, but two such rubbings in my possession are very hard to see now unless viewed obliquely because they have tarnished so badly. Another advocated the use of the lithographic crayons and lithographic transfer paper for small brasses or parts of brasses; the design could then be transferred to stone or zinc and impressions worked off them.

Finally, at the beginning of the nineteenth century Thomas Fisher, who made many fine scale drawings of brasses (especially in Bedfordshire), made use of dabbings from which he copied his final drawings. These were made using a rubber of wash leather stiffened with paper, and primed with a thin paste formed of fine black-lead powder mixed with linseed or sweet oil; the dabbings were done on strong sheets of tissue paper, and because of their frail nature were really only suitable for copying by engravers or the like. Today this same method is mainly used for reproducing indents of brasses (see pp. 51-3).

From the above description it can be seen that brass rubbings began almost at the same time as brasses (in our context) ceased to be used i.e. about 1780. Of all the various methods tried, black heel-ball was then, as now, the most popular and lasting medium. Many of the variations on the traditional method described in Chapter 3 of this book are not necessarily new – it is only the manufacturers who have changed. Those readers who think of brass rubbing as a pastime of only recent origin, may be surprised that it too has a history. One famous youthful enthusiast whose work still survives, was the young Lawrence of Arabia (see *Apollo* Vol. XXVIII (163) July, 1938).

Conclusion

To many beginners of brass rubbing the history of the brasses they have rubbed may seem irrelevant and unimportant. It will soon become clear, however, that even to those who make rubbings for decorative purposes only, some knowledge of history, heraldry, costume, armour and design will become necessary. Other people, when you show them your work, usually want to know more than just the name of the person commemorated and the date of his death. In the following pages it is hoped that some of the ideas and facts given will act as an inspiration, not only to the complete beginner, but also to those with more experience, searching for a deeper understanding and appreciation of their collection.

REFERENCES

(1) CAMERON, H. K. 'The Metals Used in Monumental Brasses.' Monumental Brass Society, Transactions Vol. VIII (4), Dec. 1946, pp. 109–130. illus. bibliog.
A very detailed article including details of the history, manufacture, processing, nomenclature, composition and analysis of brass and brasses.

(2) GADD, Margaret L. English Monumental Brasses of the Fifteenth and Early Sixteenth Centuries – with special reference (a) to the process of their manufacture and (b) to their distribution.
J. Brit. Archaeol. Assn. (3rd series), Vol. 2 (1937), pp. 17–46. maps.
An excellent paper which examines in great detail the geographical, economic and social factors influencing the manufacture and the distribution of English brasses.

(3) GAWTHORP, Walter E. 'Ancient Brass Engraving'. Notes & Queries (12th series), Vol. X, 11th March, 1922, pp. 186–187.

(4) GREENHILL, F. A. *The Incised Slabs of Leicestershire and Rutland*.
Leics. Archaeol. & Hist. Soc. 52s 6d. 1958. illus. bibliog.

(5) HARVEY, John. *The Gothic World, 1100–1600*.
Batsford. 1950. illus. bibliog. (now out of print.)

(6) JENKINS, C. K. 'Beauty In Brass'.
Apollo, August, 1946, pp. 32–34. illus.

(7) JONES, William B. 'English Monumental Brass Rubbings.'
American Artist, Vol. 24, Oct., 1960. pp. 46–49. illus.

(8) NORRIS, Malcolm. *Brass Rubbing*.
Studio Vista. 35s. 1965. illus. bibliog.

(9) *ibid* 'Mediaeval Trade in Monumental Brasses.'
Geographical Mag., Vol. XXVIII (2), March, 1956, pp. 519–525. illus.

(10) *ibid* 'Schools of Brasses in Germany.'
   J. Brit. Archaeol. Assn. (3rd series), Vol. 19 (1958). pp. 34–53. illus.

(11) WAY, Albert. 'Sepulchral Brasses, and Incised Slabs.'
   Archaeol. J. Vol. 1., Sept., 1844, pp. 197–212.

2

The Technique of Brass Rubbing: (1) Traditional Methods

Materials required. Obtaining permission. Making a rubbing. Note-taking. Rubbing mural brasses, problems of rubbing. Care of brasses when making rubbings.

(A) *Materials*

One of the chief attractions of brass rubbing as a hobby is the relatively small cost of buying the necessary materials. For convenience I will list below the essential items required by the beginner, then explain each in more detail.

Paper (minimum two rolls)
Heel-ball (minimum two sticks at any one time)
2 brushes
1 yellow duster
2 clean white cloths
Adhesive tape (two varieties)
Notebook and pencil
Folding or retracting ruler
Set of weights (optional; minimum of six)
Scissors.

(1) *Paper.* The choice of paper is very important, since it can do so much towards producing a pleasing result. Until fairly recently it was usually recommended that the beginner used a good quality white lining paper (as used

for decorating), since this is cheap and readily obtainable almost anywhere. Because it is soft, it presses well into the incised lines of most brasses, giving a generally satisfactory rubbing.

There are, however, some serious snags to using this paper, the main one being its tendency to turn yellow and brittle when displayed (or stored) for any length of time. This not only reduces the sharp black and white contrast of a new rubbing, but also the life of the rubbing itself if one wishes to build up a retrospective collection over a period of years. Other practical problems associated with this paper are its tendency to tear easily while the rubbing is underway; the thickness of the paper itself, which makes rubbing of worn or lightly engraved brasses almost impossible; and lastly, that it can be bought in one width only (22 inches), which is so often just too narrow for many compositions, making a join in the paper necessary.

For the reasons above, I would not therefore recommend any longer the use of lining paper, except as a cheap paper on which to practice, or if you do not intend to keep your rubbing for more than about two years. It is very disappointing to find a rubbing, over which you took several hours a few years previously, slowly disintegrating each time you subsequently unroll or unfold it.

Fortunately, during the last one hundred years or so, brass rubbers have had an alternative and far superior paper to the one above. Looked at today, the rubbings in some of the National collections (e.g. Society of Antiquaries; Victoria & Albert Museum) look, for the most part, as fresh and white as the day they were first made. This is because they were done on what we call today architect's detail paper. Mr Albert Way, writing in *The Archaeological Journal* of September 1844 (p. 207) says

Plate 5. Brass rubbing at Digswell Church, Hertfordshire. The author at work on the rubbing shown in Plate 8. Note how the paper is fixed with masking tape to prevent movement; how the left hand holds the paper firm near the heel-ball, and how care is being taken not to kneel on the brass itself. Much irreparable damage is done to brasses by people kneeling or standing on them when making rubbings. (*See Chapter 2.*) Photo: S. R. Oldland

Plate 6. Sir William Roberts and two wives. 1508. Little Braxted,
Essex. The owner of this well preserved Tudor brass is very
unusual in that he has an earlier brass, dated 1484 when his first
wife died, at Digswell Church, Hertfordshire. In the Digswell
example both figures are shown in burial shrouds. Three shields
above the figures are omitted from this illustration. Photo: Henry
W. Gray. Rubbing by the author

that at the time brass rubbers preferred 'a stouter and rather more expensive quality of paper, manufactured specially for the purpose of taking rubbings of brasses by Mr Limbird, 143 Strand'. It was available in widths ranging from 55 inches to 47 inches, and could be bought 'of unlimited length, like a roll of cloth'.

This paper, made basically from rag as distinct from wood pulp, can still be bought, in widths of from 30 to 60 inches, and in two qualities according to its weight. These are 50 and 70 grams per square metre, the latter, for very special rubbings, being nearly twice the price. For the beginner the price of the above paper may seen very high, since for a 25 yard roll the cost may vary from anything between 12s. 0d. and 50s. 0d., according to the weight and width. The average is between 12s. 0d. and 25s. 0d. for the size of roll most people will require, and they can be bought from many art shops, some stationers, or direct by post or by personal visit, from Phillips & Page Ltd., 50 Kensington Church St., London, S.W.1. (along with many other brass rubbing materials).

The above paper, although ideal for brass rubbing of the very best quality, is probably rather expensive for the average beginner. It must be borne in mind that 'rag paper' such as this is expensive because of the raw materials that are used in its manufacture. Fortunately, in recent years, a cheaper paper, of less weight, but offering the same advantages, has come on the market. This is a 12 yard roll of detail paper, 30 inches wide, made by Messrs Windsor & Newton Ltd., and costing (at 1968 prices) 5s. 0d. per roll. Obtainable now from many art shops, I would thoroughly recommend this to the beginner. It is well worth paying this price, although it is nearly twice that of lining paper, since the detail paper is reasonably strong and will not yellow with age. The only slight disadvantage I have found with this paper, as distinct from the expensive detail paper, is that one sometimes has to rub slightly harder with the heel-ball to get a black and even impression. This is largely due to its lighter weight, but in terms of cost alone, I think it will still be more popular with most enthusiasts. This, together with its useful width and handy size, are other advantages in its favour. A lightweight paper is also needed for the more shallowly engraved brasses, and helps bring out the detail.

(2) *Heel-ball.* With the paper, this is the next most important item in the brass rubbing kit, and must be bought with great care. There are many cheap makes on the market, most of which are wholly unsatisfactory and give very poor results. The materials that are used in its manufacture (basically bees-wax, tallow and lamp black) must be mixed in certain proportions in order for the brass rubber to obtain the darkest possible rubbing without undue wear and tear either to himself, the paper or the brass underneath. This is why it is unwise to buy a cheap variety, as many of these tend to give a blue-grey, rather than a black, finish.

In the days of hand-made and repaired boots and shoes, heel-ball (or cobbler's wax as it is sometimes known) was used a great deal to give an added lustre to the dull edges of a freshly made leather heel. In these days of machine polished shoes and compound soles and heels, heel-ball is little used for its original purpose. Today, it can still be bought at some of the smaller, and usually older, cobblers', but the best variety on the market is one specially made for the Monumental Brass Society having the brand name 'Astral'. If you are not a member of the Society itself, you can buy this heel-ball from Phillips & Page Ltd. (*op. cit.*)

for a little under 2s. 6d. per stick (minimum order four sticks if ordered by post) or in 'cake' form at 8s. 6d. each. Because this gives a very black, even rubbing, I strongly advise its use, especially if you intend to display or photograph your rubbings. The use of alternative colours (e.g. brown, white, gold) and materials (e.g. wax crayons), will be discussed in the next chapter. One final point to remember about all heel-ball, is that in warm or cold weather it can become soft and slightly sticky (making rubbing difficult and often marring fine detail), or very hard (making it more difficult to obtain an even impression). The only way to overcome this is to change to another stick, or cake, as each one becomes unworkable. The heat of the hand alone is sometimes sufficient to create the same effect.

(3) *Brushes.* Two types of brush are needed, one a fairly soft true bristle or nylon bristle for cleaning the surface of the brass free of loose grit and dust. The second, an old toothbrush or something similar, to remove pieces of grit and other matter from the incised lines of the brass itself. Do not on any account use a hard brush which could in any way damage the surface of the metal. If tears in the paper are to be eliminated, or at least minimised, a few extra minutes spent on careful brushing will reap its own rewards.

(4) *Dusters.* After brushing, a final dusting down with an ordinary household duster is recommended for removing any tiny particles which escaped the bristles. One of the dusters specially impregnated for this purpose is a useful alternative, e.g. 'Jiffytex'.

(5) *Two white cloths.* One to be used for wiping over the finished rubbing before it is removed from the brass; this gives the rubbing a good polish. The second to be used for

pressing round the main outlines of the composition, and into the incised lines of the brass itself, before the rubbing is started. This helps to locate the pieces of the brass; to minimise rubbing the surrounding stone; and to obtain a sharper contrast between the solid and white areas.

(6) *Adhesive tape.* This serves two purposes, primarily to secure the paper to the stone, wall or mounting; secondarily, to fix together sheets of paper which have to be joined. If the stone is badly pitted or powdery, tape may be of no use, in which case weights of some description must be used.

I have found two types of tape best. Masking tape, which can be removed without damage to the stone, the wall or the paper; and heavy duty plastic 'Lasso' tape (made by Smith & Nephew) which is much thicker and stronger, and will often adhere to surfaces where masking tape fails. It is not advisable to use the 'Lasso' tape for joining your paper, as it will not be easy to remove without tearing it, nor must it be used on any painted surfaces.

Should the use of any other tape be anticipated, bear in mind that many of them will leave sticky residue on the stone when peeled off; this is not only unsightly, but is not easy to remove and will not be popular with the clergy and churchwardens.

(7) *Notebook and pencil.* To be used for making on the spot notes about the brass itself (see section (C) (8) for details); or for making a preliminary sketch of the layout of the larger brasses and their accessories, so that no pieces are missed once the paper has been placed over the brass.

(8) *Ruler.* A folding or retracting ruler is essential for taking measurements for record purposes, e.g. size of slab; measurements of indents of which no rubbing is made. If a retracting ruler is bought, make sure it is one in a

square case, as brasses often get re-laid in difficult corners where a round casing will be awkward to use.

(9) *Set of weights*. If these can be made (and transported) they will prove very useful for holding the paper down firmly. The alternative is to use hassocks (which usually make the paper dirty) or masking tape, which will some-times not adhere to the slab. A minimum of six weights is necessary.

(10) *Scissors*. For general purposes such as cutting lengths of paper from a roll, cutting pieces of adhesive tape, etc.

(B) Obtaining permission

Although it should not be necessary to state here that it is only courteous to make every effort to obtain permission to rub a brass, incumbents frequently complain of abuse of this privilege. In most cases, once applied for, permission is readily given. It is not uncommon now for churches to make a nominal charge for rubbing their brasses, the amount usually depending on the fame of the brasses concerned. It may vary from anything between a verbal request to 'place a contribution in the box as you leave', to a fixed charge of up to 30s. 0d.; 5s. 0d. and 7s. 6d. are probably the most common charges that will be met with. The practice of making a charge for rubbings will also be encountered abroad, but there are, as in this country, still many churches where no fee is stipulated.

If you cannot find the incumbent, and in remoter districts or where several parishes are administered by one man this not uncommon, try finding a churchwarden, the verger or the person who holds the key should the church be locked. He/she may be able to help you and indeed will often welcome an enquiry. If the brass is especially famous, e.g. Stoke D'Abernon, Trumpington, it is necessary and indeed far better to write first, as a booking will almost certainly be required. This will help not only you, since it will save you unecessary disappointment if you are refused because of a full day's bookings, but will help the church officers who obviously have other demands on their building besides brass rubbing. In some instances, you may even find permission is refused except in very exceptional circumstances, this usually being because demand far exceeds the time available, or because the brass(es) is (are) in danger of becoming damaged by any further rubbing. In a few cases permission is only given to members of the Monumental Brass Society, provided application is made in writing first. The famous series of brasses at Cobham, Kent are one example where rubbing is no longer possible.

The Universities – If you wish to rub any of the brasses in the College chapels at Oxford and Cambridge, application should be made in the first instance (and preferably in writing) to the Office of the appropriate College Principal, e.g. The Warden, The President, The Master; or in some cases to the College Chaplain or his Clerk. Since practice differs from one College to another, you will probably find it safest to check in the University Handbook or Calendar at your local Reference Library, as to the exact designation of the Principal if you intend writing first.

Abroad – Brass rubbing abroad presents its own particular problems, not least of which is that of language.

On the whole you will find the church and museum authorities very co-operative, the biggest problem being to find the person in authority. Again, it is sometimes better to write first as you may find your expedition clashes with a religious festival or some other activity. A useful little pamphlet issued by the Monumental Brass Society and written by M. W. Norris and Dr H. K. Cameron, called *Brief Notes Concerning Monumental Brasses on the Continent of Europe*, offers very sound advice and I would recommend those going abroad to obtain it. It can be bought from the Hon. Sec. of the Society for 2s. 6d. (plus 4d. postage). In addition to general guidance, it also gives a few notes on brasses which were destroyed during the last war, or have been subsequently moved to new positions, e.g. into museums. Do not rely for information on an old list.

When you go abroad, remember that many of the brasses are very large, so ensure that you have a plentiful supply of all the necessary materials, especially heel-ball and wide detail paper. You may be able to buy the paper (even if in a narrower width) but is it very unlikely that you will find any heel-ball, though a good wax crayon may be obtainable as a substitute should the worst happen. Far better in the long run to take too much than too little of everything, since you are sure to run out in the most inaccessible place you visit!

(C) *Making a rubbing by the traditional method*

Having now obtained the necessary materials and permission to make your rubbing, it is then time to locate the brass you wish to rub first. Unless the brass and/or its slab have been moved at some later date, most of the brasses laid down before about 1470 were either on the floor of the church or on a raised tomb. From the brass rubber's point of view this is perhaps fortunate, as mural brasses are usually the most difficult to rub because of the problem of fixing the paper satisfactorily. There can be no general rule as to where in the church you will find the brasses, as so many factors may decide its site, e.g. actual number of brasses already *in situ;* the rank of the person commemorated; whether or not the slab has been subsequently moved. It is for the more unusual places that one has to be on the look-out, e.g. on window-sills; in vestries; under platforms; high up on the wall or even outside the church itself in a few cases.

Fortunately, as most of the brasses are still situated on the floors of churches, I will deal with these first and add a few notes on the special problems of mural brasses afterwards. For ease of reference I will set out main points numerically below, in approximately their order of operation:

(1) Remove any matting or other covering over the brass, making a brief mental note of how it was arranged if there are several pieces; similarly any pieces of furniture, platforms, etc.

(2) If the brass has many accessories, i.e. shields, scrolls, groups of children, canopy work, it is advisable to make a rough sketch in your note-book of the relation of the various parts. This is so that no pieces are missed once the paper is fixed down or has been removed once the rubbing is finished.

(3) Clean the brass and surrounding area very carefully with your brush and duster (including the incised lines of the brass itself, especially if they are particularly deep or wide) to remove any loose grit and dust that has invariably collected on the surface. If the brass has a marginal inscription, clean as much of the slab inside this area as well. This is essential if one wishes to avoid unnecessary tears in the paper, as when you are rubbing with heel-ball especially, the pressure of the rubbing action over even a

small piece of grit can be disastrous and may well ruin several hours work on a larger composition.

(4) Unroll your paper until the brass is completely covered, leaving a fairly generous margin of waste above and below the extremities of the composition. This allows both for fixing the paper down and for trimming after the work is completed. Cut the required length(s) of paper from the roll. If the brass happens to be wider than your paper it will be necessary to join two (or very rarely, three) lengths. If possible do this in such a way as to get as little of the join over the brass itself (an obvious case where this is not possible is on the large Flemish brasses which display one solid area of brass). Overlap the join as little as possible unless it falls mainly on the slab itself and fix the pieces at as many points as is practicable to obtain maximum adhesion and minimum movement. If the pieces are to be permanently joined afterwards (i.e. glued together) try and use a tape such as masking tape which can be removed later with a minimum of damage to the paper.

(5) Secure your paper firmly down, either using tape as in (4) above (but not sellotape as this will not usually adhere if there is any powdering of the stone and because it is hard to remove, leaving a dirty mark behind afterwards) or, if the slab is too pitted or rough for tape, use weights of some description. These can be hassocks, if available, or if nothing else is to hand and you have no weights of your own, a few hymn books might be sufficient for small brasses. If you use any church property, and I do not think you should if you come properly prepared, remember to replace anything you borrow afterwards. A few heavy books from your own home would do equally well if you can transport them.

(6) Locate each part of the brass, either by using your preliminary sketch, or by tapping the stone with the blunt end of a pencil until you hear it strike the metal (the latter method will not work so well if the brass is very firmly fixed in its matrix). With your clean cloth, press round the outline of the various parts, and into the incised lines of the brass itself where possible. The former helps you to avoid rubbing over the edge of the brass and on to the stone too often; the latter helps to give a better contrast between the two tones provided the incised lines are not still full of bitumen or similar filling. On a large composition the paper may stretch as you work down the brass, so do not be surprised if your first outline does not quite match when you get near the end of your rubbing.

(7) Make sure, if you are using a stick of heel-ball, that the end is fairly blunt, for a pointed piece will tend to go into the incised lines of the brass and blurr the image. Now begin your rubbing. The order in which you rub the various parts is optional and is often governed by the position of the brass itself in relation to its surroundings. Normal practice is to work from the top to the bottom of the composition, but you may choose to rub, say, the figure and foot-inscription first, leaving any groups of children and any other accessories, e.g. shields, scrolls, until last. Work however you find it most convenient, but be careful not to miss anything out – if you think you might, then make a rough sketch before starting.

If your heel-ball and paper are of good quality, you should not have to press too hard (though do not expect it to be effortless), firm strokes of even pressure are all that are needed. Try and obtain equal contrast throughout; most people prefer to rub using an up and down action, but there will be times when a variety of directions may be necessary, e.g. when rivets protrude above the surface of the metal.

One of the most difficult problems facing any brass rubber is that of going as little off the edge of the brass as possible. The fact that some of the surrounding stone has been rubbed does not worry some people, and as will be mentioned later, the necessity of mounting or not mounting rubbings is basically an aesthetic one. If the rubbing is very large, it may not be worth the extra and painstaking effort of mounting it, which is the one obvious way of getting rid of the overlap. The problem is increased when the brass lies below the surface of the stone matrix. Whilst I do not favour mounting unless the rubbing is purely for decorative purposes, past experience has also proved that the finished result, unless done very carefully, is not always better to look at, since it is quite difficult to get all the parts exactly square and in their original position. This is why rubbings done for historical purposes must always be unmounted.

When you have finished your rubbing, do not forget to rub it over with your second cloth to give it a final polish. This cannot be done satisfactorily once the rubbing has been removed. Having rolled up your paper and put away your materials, remember to replace any mats, pieces of furniture and other objects belonging to the church. Heel-ball tends to leave a large number of flakes during rubbing, so if possible, try and collect these into something, rather than leaving them lying all over the floor around the brass. These extra few minutes spent cleaning up can do so much towards creating goodwill between the clergy and brass rubbing enthusiasts.

(8) Notes: It is good practice to cultivate a systematic method for recording notes about each rubbing. These

will not only help you to remember details a few weeks later should you not catalogue your rubbing straight away, but are essential if your rubbings and records are to be of any permanent value as historical records in years to come. Although you may never intend, or even anticipate, that your rubbings will ever find their way into national or local archive collections, make accurate notes none the less if you are intending to amass a collection of any size. One day, some researcher may find your rubbings and/or notes useful, just as we today find rubbings, impressions and drawings, etc., taken by the first collectors (many of brasses since lost or damaged) of such inestimable value, e.g. Society of Antiquaries; British Museum and Victoria & Albert Museum collections (*op. cit.*).

Cataloguing and indexing a collection will be dealt with in Chapter 4, but the following basic information should be recorded on the spot:

Location	e.g. St John the Evangelist, Digswell, Herts.
Date rubbing made	
Position of brass	e.g. Sanctuary; north side.
Identification of brass	e.g. Sir John Peryent and wife Joan. 1415.
Special features (if any)	e.g. Re-laid in new slab; slab re-used in 1796 with following inscription . . .
Indents (if any)	Include measurements if no rubbing or dabbing made; note relation to rest of brass/slab.
Size of slab	Include original and/or new slab; if moved and old slab survives, record all details of latter including its position.

Mural brasses

As mentioned earlier, taking rubbings of mural brasses (including those found on the panels of canopied altar tombs) present special problems. The main one is that of fixing the paper to the wall, or panel, itself. The other one is the sheer physical effort of doing the rubbing, which can be extremely tiring when the brass is at an awkward height or very large.

Many brasses which are now mural have been placed on the wall at a later date, usually as a better means of preserving them. Sometimes they are mounted on wooden boards (e.g. Gt Berkhamsted, Herts.); at other times they are re-fixed at almost inaccessible heights, e.g. at Hinxworth, Herts. a civilian and his wife of *c*. 1450, have at some date been re-fixed to an oval stone and placed about twelve feet up on the chancel wall!

Fixing the paper to rub any mural brass depends almost entirely for its success on the type of surface to which the brass is fixed. Wooden boards, smooth stone or concrete slabs which have not become pitted or powdery can usually be coped with by using masking tape. Do not use sellotape for the reasons already given in section (A).

(9) If the stone or wall is rough, powdery or badly damaged, the heavy duty 'Lasso' tape may work, but if this fails to adhere there is little choice but to try and find somebody who is willing to hold the paper in position as best they can, whilst you make your rubbing. Remember, however, that this is very tiring too, so do not try it on too large a brass for either your sakes! Fortunately, most of the brasses which are original mural brasses are of later date (*c*. 1470 onwards) and tend to be fairly small.

The care of brasses.

A special note must be added here on the great import-ance of exercising great care when making brass rubbings. With the growing numbers of people making rubbings themselves the brasses are more and more prone to damage. This usually occurs when pieces of the brass work loose, resulting in cracks or fractures in the metal caused by the weight of people kneeling or standing on the edges. I cannot stress too strongly how important it is to avoid this practice, knowingly or otherwise. In an increasing number of churches all brass rubbing has had to be stopped because of damage done, or likely to be done, by those unaware of the above facts.

3

The Technique of Brass Rubbing: (2) Alternative Methods

New materials, crayons, colours. Reverse rubbings. Dabbings. 'Rubbings' on aluminium foil.

(A) New materials

In recent years an increasing number of alternative methods and materials for brass rubbing have become available. Amongst these are a variety of different coloured heel-ball, crayons and papers, and 'rubbings' on aluminium foil.

Heel-ball can now be obtained from Messrs. Phillips & Page Ltd. in red, gold, brown and white. The first three are ideal for experimenting with using gold or more especially black paper; red on white paper is also quite pleasing. The 'Astral' white heel-ball is unsuitable for use with black paper as it lacks density, but can be used for the 'reverse' method of rubbing described below; for rubbings in white on black paper, a crayon is preferable.

Crayons have always been available for artists, and experiments have proved that some of these can be used to great effect for brass rubbings. To describe all the variations possible and the variety of colours available would be both boring and unnecessary, as they can be seen readily enough in any art shop. I will, however, list a small number which I have used and found to be effective, but readers must largely decide for themselves those which they like best. Prices given are those at the time of publication, and are intended only as a guide.

Black
> Harbutt's 'Acorn' Crayons (4d. each) – best on cheaper detail paper.
> Rowney New Art Crayons (5d. each, or in boxes of 9 and 12 assorted colours).
> Hardtmuth Black No. 65C.
> Summit Wax (1s. 2d. stick).

White
> Harbutt's 'Acorn' Crayons.
> 'Finart' wax crayons (usually available in box of 16 mixed colours only).

Gold
> A. W. Faber – Castell (Germany) 'Colorex' No. 2987A. (1s. 0d. each).
> Available singly or in box of 6 (cost 6s. 0d. per box). Six metallic pastels of the following shades are offered:
> No. 49 (Silver)
> No. 50–53 (four shades of Gold)
> No. 54 (Copper)
> Although these are mainly suitable for smaller brasses they make very attractive rubbings on black paper. The brass chosen must be fairly deeply engraved or the detail will be lost because of the chalky nature of the pastels. You will also find that the pastel will bend or even break when you are making the rubbing because it softens in the heat of the hand. After completing the rubbing it is best to use a fixative to avoid possible smudging of the chalk. Other colours are also available in the same range.

Plate 7.
Elizabeth Parker.
1602. Radwell,
Hertfordshire. Late
Elizabethan brasses like this
one are well drawn,
excessively shaded to try
and give dimension to the
figure and very hard to rub
because the thin metal of the
original is often badly
dented. As in this example
inscriptions present
particular difficulties. (*See
Chapter 2.*) Photo: S. R.
Oldland. Rubbing by the
author

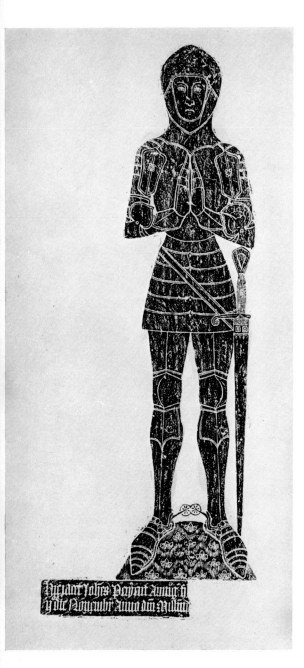

Plate 8.
Sir John Peryent (jnr).
1442. Digswell,
Hertfordshire. Figures of
this size make excellent
rubbings for decoration in
the home, either in black
and white or in colour
(especially gold). This
particular example (some 3
ft high) shows equally well
the simple yet accurate
method of depicting armour
on brasses. Photo: Henry
W. Gray. Rubbing by the
author

Other Colours

Hardtmuth Crayons offer a wide range of colours of which the best for brass rubbing purposes are yellow (No. 65E); Red (No. 65A) and Brown (No. 65F); blue and green are also available, but I do not find either very useful even for decorative purposes. The possible use of a set of different coloured crayons (e.g. Finart, Rowney) for colouring heraldic brasses or shields of Arms is feasible, though very time consuming. If a light pencil 'rubbing' is made first, it is possible to colour in the tinctures of the Arms either immediately, or later on at home if this is easier (another alternative is to use poster paints). A very interesting book by the Heraldry Society called *The Colour of Heraldry* (Pub. by the Society in 1958) will give a very good idea of the variety and splendour of colours possible on church brasses and tombs. I have found that, generally speaking, most colours look more effective on black paper rather than white.

Paper

The only coloured papers I have seen which are suitable for brass rubbing are gold and matt black. Both these are available from *Phillips & Page Ltd. in 10 yard rolls of 30 inch width, the gold costing about twice as much as the black. A black detail paper made by Windsor and Newton can be bought in some shops, either in rolls, costing about 17s. 6d., or occasionally by the yard. Of the two, I find the black infinitely more useful. Other colours may become

*Mr Page-Phillips tells me that he is about to market (July 1968) a brass rubbing bookcloth in rolls 7 feet long by 40 inches wide, at 11s. 0d. per roll. This will be available in black, white, dark and light blue, red, yellow, aubergine and green. A more expensive, tougher bookcloth is also available in short lengths for those wishing to make unmounted rubbings.

available in time, and I have seen one fairly successful experiment made on a paper coloured with a wash of red poster paint, then used to make the traditional black rubbing.

(B) *'Reverse' method of rubbing*

To many people this may prove an exacting and difficult task, but if it can be mastered successfully a really fine effect can be achieved. For ease of explanation, I will enumerate the basic principles of this method below, and I would advise anybody trying this for the first time to choose a relatively simple, small design before embarking on a complicated or larger composition. The idea behind this method is to produce either a 'positive' rubbing with black lines only, and/or, to produce a coloured facsimile.

(1) Using 'Astral' white heel-ball (or a poor quality unbranded heel-ball, e.g. brown) make your rubbing on detail paper in the normal way. If only the coats of Arms are being coloured, then the figures and other accessories could perhaps be done in gold or the traditional black. Choose a brass which does not have too much fine detail but which is none the less clearly engraved.

(2) Take your rubbing home, and using waterproof ink, black in the lines of the brass very carefully, and allow the ink to dry thoroughly. The lining in is very important and must be done well to give a good finished effect.

(3) Using a clean rag soaked in paraffin or lighter fuel, wipe over the areas covered by the heel-ball; the spirit will make the surface of the heel-ball flake and disintegrate. Do not do this too near direct heat or a naked flame, and preferably do not smoke.

(4) Allow the paper to dry thoroughly, preferably over-night.

(5) Determine the correct tinctures of the parts to be

coloured (a County History or General Armoury might help with coats of Arms). Using either waterproof ink, poster colours or, for a 'softer' appearance ordinary pencil crayons, colour in the tinctures as appropriate; unless every trace of the wax in the heel-ball has been removed application of colour might prove difficult, and a coating of ox-gall may help to remove the 'greasiness' from the paper. As with the lining in, this part of the operation requires some skill and patience, but is well worth the effort if it is successful.

(6) If necessary, cut out and mount the finished work. (*See Pl. 9.*)

(C) *Dabbings*

Although few beginners are likely to use 'dabbings', a short note on their function and method of production is necessary. Their purpose is chiefly as a medium for taking impressions of indents of brasses and parts of brasses, showing their relationship to the existing brass, which can also be copied in the same way. It is used mainly for historical record purposes, but adaptations can be made for decorative work as well.

The usual method of operation is as follows:

(1) Make an absorbent pad from a piece of chamois leather and cotton wool, placing the latter inside the piece of leather.

(2) Obtain some powdered graphite (which is unfortunately not always easy to buy commercially, but can be made from a thick piece of artist's graphite crayon suitably ground down) and a small bottle of linseed oil. Mix the two into a fairly stiff paste on an old tin lid or a small piece of wooden or formica type board, using a pallet knife.

(3) Using tissue paper (obtainable from Phillips &

Page Ltd., or some stationers and art shops) lay this over the brass and slab in the normal way, pressing it gently into the lines of the brass itself (where it survives) and/or round the outline of the indents of the missing pieces. The thin Windsor & Newton white detail paper can be used instead, but even this is a little thick to produce a clear impression.

(4) Dip the pad into the paste, wipe off any surplus on to the board, and apply to the paper. Press the pad firmly on to the paper, avoiding any rubbing movement as this will move the paper. Continuing in this way, gradually cover the whole slab until all the necessary parts have been reproduced. Where there are indents, ensure that only the outside edges are dabbed leaving the indented parts white, except to show the positions of the studs or stud holes which should be carefully located. The latter process, which is not always easy once the paper is in position, can be omitted if the dabbing is not for historical use. An article on dabbings can be seen in the M.B.S. Trans. Vol. 7 (1934–42) pp. 290–93.

(5) Dabbings will not be as black as heel-ball rubbings, and if the slab is a large one, or not in good condition, can take a considerable time. For this reason they are not generally popular with all but the most ardent enthusiast.

It would not be out of place just to mention here the importance of indents, the recording of which are every bit as vital, historically speaking, as the existing brasses. Since slabs without any pieces of brass remaining tend to get destroyed during any restoration of the church (especially if the floor is relaid) and also wear away more easily, the accurate recording of them is a very important task. This is probably one of the most neglected aspects of research into brasses still remaining to be done, but the task is a forbidding one when the number involved is considered – about 8,000 would be a conservative estimate. The Monumental Brass Society is at present (1968) trying to gather a team of people to assist in recording all the indents of brasses in this country and abroad, with a view to publishing a complete list.

(D) *'Rubbings' on aluminium foil*

This is an entirely new technique discovered only recently by two American scientists while engaged on research work in this country. Drs Thomas Reed and William Street decided to try and discover a new method of producing a 'positive' reproduction instead of the traditional 'negative' result obtained with black heel-ball. They did this using 50 micron aluminium foil – not the type used in cooking but more like that used for milk bottle tops. Their method is as follows:

(1) Lay the foil over the brass and obtain an impression using a soft nail brush. By rubbing this over the aluminium, the foil will be pressed into the incised lines of the brass underneath. This process will only take a few minutes on a small brass, but before removing the foil check to see that you have obtained an even impression over the whole area. Remove the foil, cut it from the roll and very carefully wind it on to a cardboard tube, trying to avoid unnecessary creases in the foil as much as possible.

(2) (a) Once home, lay the foil face down on a flat surface, and apply several coats of sodium silicate – 'waterglass' (e.g. Mangers) – allowing each coat to dry and harden before applying the next. This will take several hours and is the longest part of the operation.

(b) An alternative method but more expensive, is to use fibreglas resin to coat the back of the foil. This can then be stuck straight on to a fibreglas or hardboard backing. If you use resin, be sure to do your coating on something which you do not require afterwards, as it is very sticky and not easily removed.

(3) Fill in the lines of the impression by rubbing over it with cotton wool or rag dipped in liquid shoe black or silk screen ink. Remove any surplus by rubbing gently over the 'white' areas with a fine steel wool.

(4) If method 2. (b) is not used to mount the foil, then an alternative is to cut out your 'rubbing' and mount it on a piece of hardboard using a quick drying adhesive (e.g. P.V.A. emulsion) around the edges. The backing board could be painted with a matt black (or dark) paint to give a good contrast.

At the time of writing the special foil for use with this method was obtainable only by direct application to the Aluminium Federation, Portland House, Stag Place, London, S.W.1., in about 20 ft. rolls, 24 inches wide (price 5s. 0d. post free). Supplies of these are, however, limited and the amount of work involved may well deter many people. I am greatly indebted to the Federation for much of the information given above, the first details of which were published in their leaflet 'Aluminium for Schools' of Summer Term, 1967. Variations on the process may yet be discovered, but at the present time the method above is the only one known to the author. The two illustrations shown give a good idea of the effect produced, the metallic appearance of the original brass being almost preserved. Unfortunately, it is very difficult to prevent the backing material from showing through the foil in some areas, but further experiments may eliminate this in due course. A great deal of credit is due to the two post-graduates who discovered this unique process. (*See Pl. 10 and 11.*)

4

The Display and Storage of Rubbings

Display in the home. Mounting rubbings. Photographing
rubbings. Screen printing from rubbings. Public exhibitions of
rubbings. Facsimiles of brasses. Storage of rubbings. Cataloguing
a collection. Indexing a collection.

(A) Display

(1) *In the home*. Most readers of the book will probably
have seen the many commercially produced prints and
reproductions of brasses. Today one can buy greetings
cards, table mats, lampshades, bookmarks, prints for
framing on paper, card and suede, all portraying brasses to
varying degrees of success. Some London and large provincial shops sell actual brass rubbings, often at quite
inflated prices. Many of the above items are good, others
extremely poor and it seems a great pity to me that
brasses should have become so much a part of commercial
enterprise. In many cases the churches themselves receive
nothing in return from the manufacturers, as there is no
law to protect them from reproduction of their brasses for
profit. Personally, I obtain far more satisfaction from a
rubbing I have done myself.

Displaying rubbings in one's own home has obvious
limitations, usually imposed by the space available.
Whether your rubbings are of the traditional type, or done
in colour for purely decorative purposes, the principles
explained below apply to all of them. I shall speak only in

very general terms, so it must be borne in mind that many adaptations are possible, and may well be preferred to the methods listed below.

Framing with or without glass is almost self-explanatory, but for most homes only fairly small brasses will be feasible. Large frames and sheets of glass are expensive and added to this is the cost of a hardboard or wooden base on which the rubbing must be mounted. If glass is used, bear in mind that from many angles it may reflect patches of light, unless it is very carefully positioned on the wall. If a large, unglazed, rubbing can be displayed in a suitable frame above, say, a fireplace, the effect can be just as striking as the coloured panoramas one sees in many modern homes. Large blank areas of wall such as this, or on staircases and landings, lend themselves very well to large rubbings, and are very sought after in American homes. It is the lighting of them that requires the most skill. Rubbings too, have a shiny surface and unfortunately it is not possible to matsil them as the heat melts the wax in the heel-ball or crayon. Remember also to use a paper like detail paper for your rubbing which will not turn yellow when exposed to light for long periods.

A cheaper method of displaying rubbings is simply to fix a bamboo or flat wooden baton to each end of the paper, attach a picture cord or chain to the top baton and hang the rubbing just as it is. Alternatively, the rubbing could be cut out and re-mounted on a stiffer white or coloured paper or card and then hung in the same way. Other useful backing materials are canvas, white calico and hardboard; for wall hangings the latter has limitations of size, but calico is a very useful general purpose material which can be used to reinforce any displayed or special rubbings; its main limitation for general use is purely one of cost.

For any kind of mounting it is very important to use the correct adhesive and if in any doubt seek professional advice first. On the whole I prefer unmounted rubbings, but for those who are going to back their paper by one of the methods above the following points should be remembered. Many pastes when they dry out have a tendency to crease the paper, especially if complete adhesion has not occurred over the whole surface, i.e. air pockets have formed, as happens all too often with wallpaper. If a water based paste is used, e.g. flour and water, wallpaper paste, these make the paper very wet and fragile, but have the advantage of not drying on contact so that the rubbing can be positioned correctly before being fixed down. The two disadvantages I have found with flour and water paste (which can of course be made at home quite cheaply) are (1) it attracts mice and 'paper eating' bacteria if the rubbings are not stored correctly and (2) over a long period of time it has a tendency to produce a white dusty fungus on the surface of the rubbing; this can be easily wiped away, but is none the less a nuisance. Wallpaper pastes have the advantage here as they are usually fungus resistant, but they are very slow drying. As alternatives to the above one can try a P.V.A. adhesive (which again is rather slow to dry), one of the special glues used for photographic mounting (provided the rubbing is not too large as these tend to be rather expensive) or, again in the case of smaller compositions only, 'Cow' gum Copydex or something similar, where almost instant adhesion is required. If these are used make sure there are no lumps under your paper before you press it down, and bear in mind that in quantity, such adhesives are rather expensive.

It will be clear from the above comments that there is

no ideal adhesive, and one must decide by experiment which is most suited to individual needs. Wallpaper pastes (e.g. Polycell, Rex) offer the most advantages over the others and are relatively cheap, economic and easy to use; they also dry without marking the paper which is equally important. If a proprietary brand is used, make sure it is mixed and applied according to the manufacturers instructions, or a treasured rubbing may be ruined.

(2) *Photographing brass rubbings.* Anybody who has tried to photograph a brass rubbing will appreciate that it is not as simple as it might appear. Unless the lighting is arranged correctly and the camera placed so that the optical axis meets the exact centre of the rubbing and is at right angles to it, a blurred or distorted image will result. If a tripod is used, and it will almost certainly be necessary to obtain a good image, ensure that it is absolutely rigid; a centre column tripod is the most satisfactory in this respect and helps squaring up as well.

Even lighting is often best achieved by photographing your rubbing out of doors, though too strong or too dull a light will again produce bad images. Because brass rubbings are shiny, they reflect directional lighting, therefore evenly diffused light is necessary. In addition, if the rubbing has been mounted, creases, not apparent from a distance, will blur the image or cause unevenness, especially if angled lighting is used, e.g. artificial light. The ideal day for outdoor work is soft daylight with overcast skies. If you use light indoors, choose a room where you can place your rubbing centrally with windows of about equal size in two opposing walls. If the room only has one window, place your rubbing some distance from it to avoid too much directional light and allow for the reduction in lighting by increasing your exposure time. In a room with one window and rather dark decoration some kind of reflector may be necessary (e.g. a large card or piece of board covered with aluminium foil; a large mirror) to compensate for any falling off of illumination from one side.

Artificial lighting is probably the more difficult to arrange, largely because of the shiny surface of the original rubbing. One lamp will not be satisfactory and depending on the size of the rubbing, two, or preferably four lamps, will be required. These can be either fluorescent tubes or normal lamps with reflectors. These should be directed in such a way as to give evenly diffused light over the whole surface of the paper and placed at an angle of about 50–60 degrees to the optical axis, or about 30–40 degrees to the original.

The choice of film for black and white originals is not terribly important, but try and obtain a fine grain film with a fairly thick emulsion, since this will achieve far better contrast and reproduction of the finer detail often met with on brasses. If you are photographing a rubbing for block making purposes print your negative on to fairly fine grained paper, and glaze the surface of the print as this gives greater contrast than a matt finish.

Once you have made a satisfactory negative it can be used in any number of ways other than for straight copying. Parts of the brass can be enlarged, e.g. the figure of a saint in a canopy or on the orphrey of a cope, and printed for use as personal bookmarks, greetings cards, etc. Using reversal methods the incised lines only of the brass can be reproduced as is done for line block illustrations in books and periodicals.

Slides can also be made following similar principles to those noted above and can be produced by direct copy or using a negative in the usual way. Instead of printing on to paper, film is used, which when processed can produce a positive transparency. Slides are ideal when giving talks where display facilities are restricted and apart from saving wear and tear on the original rubbings, means that many of the larger brasses can be shown to good effect. The only possible criticism of using slides that I can think of is that they do not give the layman a true idea of the size and magnificence of some of the original brasses, but this is purely a technicality. The best solution is a combination of both slides and rubbings.

One other great advantage of a transparency is that it can be made from almost any original, including reproductions in books and periodicals where no infringement of copyright is being made. This means that you can illustrate your talk with illustrations of brasses of which you have no original rubbings yourself.

For those who wish to make a hobby of photographing rubbings I would recommend their reading the relevant parts of a book by O. R. Croy called *Camera Copying and Reproduction* (Focal Press. 37s. 6d. 1964), especially the chapters entitled 'Aims and Means' (pp. 65–67 in particular) and 'Illumination' (pp. 93–100 in particular). I have found this to be of great value, especially as it is clear, concise and not too technical for the average enthusiast.

(3) *Screen prints*. The use of brass rubbings for screen prints is a new technique and is one which those with easy access to the proper equipment will find simplest. The equipment described below can, however, be home-made, but for those not so inclined it can be bought at most art shops as well. As I have been unable to find any description of the use of brass rubbings for screen printing this section should prove of interest to many schools, Colleges of

Further Education, Art Schools and Colleges of Education, who will already possess the equipment required.

For those unable to obtain professional instructions, I would recommend them to buy the pamphlet *Simple Screen Printing* by Anthony Kinsey (Dryad Press. 7s. 6d. 1968) or the same author's earlier book *Introducing Screen Printing* (Batsford. 30s. 0d. 1967). These will give you fuller details than those outlined below, plus a short list of suppliers of equipment. The method I am describing in outline is only one of several adaptations of the process, but one which I think will give the beginner an added interest in his collection of rubbings.

If you experiment first with the simplest techniques described by Mr Kinsey this will help you to master the 'photographic' method far more confidently. To begin with the following basic equipment and materials are required:

(a) Wooden screen frame (this can be home-made and the size can be varied to suit one's own requirements).

(b) Enough cotton organdie to give three layers over the frame.

(c) Tin (or jar) of (a) photographic gelatine and (b) potassium dichromate.

(d) Soft brush, e.g. 3 inch soft bristle paint brush.

(e) Sheet of clear glass large enough to more than cover your wooden frame, the heavier weight of glass the better; allow about $1\frac{1}{2}$–2 inches overlap.

(f) Roll of sellotape.

(g) Wooden board which will fit inside your screen frame.

(h) Something on which to support (g) above, e.g. books, a box, bricks.

(i) Short length of rubber or plastic hose.

(j) Access to hot running water.

(k) Somewhere dark to store the prepared screen.

(l) A brass rubbing on detail paper.

(m) Bottle of turpentine.

(n) 2 inch wide gumstrip (paper or p.v.c. tape).

(o) Box of large drawing pins.

This may seem rather a formidable list at first glance, but in fact few of these items are expensive and some can be home-made; the wooden screen frame (if not home-made) is probably the largest single expenditure likely to be incurred.

Method

Prepare your screen by fixing the organdie over one side of the frame, securing the material as tightly as possible at the sides with plenty of drawing pins. Three layers of organdie are needed and care must be taken not to stretch them so tight as to tear them during fixing. Paper gumstrip or p.v.c. adhesive tape of at least 2 inches in width is then placed round each side of the frame to form a printing area of the size required.

Dissolve the gelatine in hot (but not boiling) water (mix according to manufacturer's instructions) by placing it in a fairly large, clean tin or similar receptacle. Then, using your brush, paint the liquid gelatine over the organdie, getting as even a coating as possible. Cover every part of the surface very carefully, making sure you do not leave any air bubbles on the material as these will spoil your final print.

Once the gelatine is dry, the surface can then be coated with potassium dichromate. This must be done in a darkened room away from direct light, since the mixture becomes light sensitive as soon as it is dry. Perform this part of the operation as quickly as possible, storing your

62

screen in a dark room or cupboard for at least ten hours, preferably overnight for the most part. The screen must be completely dry before it is used or the process will not work.

Before you can use your rubbing, it is best to rub turpentine, or thin lubricating oil, over the whole surface of the detail paper as this helps to make it more transparent. Also, because the white areas then become transluscent, not only is a better contrast obtained when printing, but the texture of the original rubbing is reproduced to great effect. (*vide* illustration f.p. 81.)

Having prepared your rubbing, fix it to the sheet of glass with sellotape, making sure that it fits into the inside measurements of your frame since the tape was added. It is best to begin with not to be over-ambitious and work with a screen more than about $2\frac{1}{2}$–3 feet long. Place the board cut to fit the inside of the screen on the pile of books, bricks, etc. Bring out your prepared screen, preferably in a room where the curtains have been drawn if it is daytime. Place the screen over the board above with the prepared side uppermost, then quickly lay the glass with its rubbing underneath, on top of the screen, so that the black areas block out any light. Check to make sure you have fixed your rubbing to the glass correctly so that it will not print back to front. The whole equipment can then be placed in a window, or under strong artificial light, the latter taking longer to work than the former. Because the rubbing, however black, is never opaque give the screen a very short exposure (about three to five minutes) or you will lose clarity in the image. Soon the potassium dichromate will gradually turn from orange-yellow to a lightish brown, by which time the process is complete.

When the screen is ready, wash it down with warm water to remove the gelatine which was covered by the black areas of the rubbing. The screen can then be dried and an exact reproduction of the original will be visible. This can now be printed using the normal screen printing methods.

(4) *Exhibitions.* The effective staging of an exhibition of privately owned rubbings is no easy matter. One of the greatest problems is that of finding a suitable hall which allows the rubbings to be well spaced and yet viewable from a reasonable distance. Unless only smaller brasses are chosen, the considerable size of many brasses impose further limitations. If you have spent a number of years carefully collecting a series of rubbings of the best brasses, it is worth making a special effort to find a good hall or gallery in which to exhibit them.

Many of the larger public libraries, civic halls and schools offer suitable exhibition spaces and I have also mounted one exhibition in a large parish church, where even the great Flemish brasses could be displayed to great effect. For many readers of this book, however, a village hall, scout or guide hut may be the only local facility available, but provided your rubbings are clean, well mounted and hung and are catalogued and labelled clearly, then half the battle is won. If you do produce an accompanying catalogue or list, and it is certainly preferable to do so, make sure the numbers in the catalogue do actually relate to those identifying each rubbing. This may sound obvious, but if other people are helping you to mount the exhibition because time is short, some strange mistakes can occur. Aim at a helpful arrangement, so that as far as possible the visitors can walk round in a fairly logical fashion, following the numbers in sequence as they go.

Plate 9. Rev. Richard Folcard. 1451. Pakefield, Suffolk. A good example of a reverse rubbing produced by the method described in Chapter 3(B). With patience, this time consuming process can be very rewarding; the example above took about five hours to complete, of which over half was spent on the inscription.

Photo: Henry W. Gray. Rubbing by the author

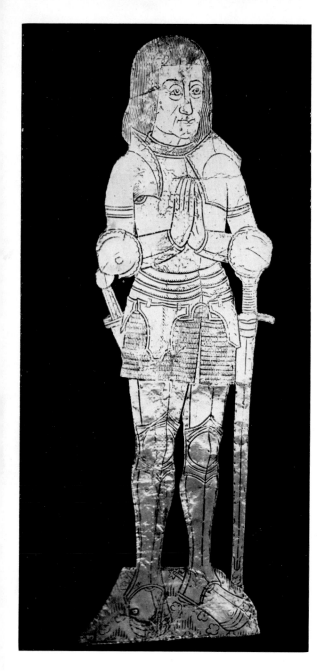

Plate 10.
Knight. _c._ 1500.
This excellent example of
an aluminium foil 'rubbing'
was made by the two
American post-graduates
who discovered the process.
Note how well this 'positive'
rubbing reproduces the
engraved lines of the
original brass.
(_See Chapter 3._)
Photo: Aluminium
Federation

If time, and money, permit, the entries in the catalogue should have brief informative notes where appropriate. This may vary in length from three or four lines to a dozen lines or so, according to the size of the exhibition and the space you can afford in your catalogue. One pleasing, but not too expensive, method of production is to type the catalogue or list on to metal or plastic offset litho stencils, which can then be printed in larger numbers than the traditional stencil. If a good sans serif face is used, this can look very attractive provided the page layout is correct. Quarto paper (8 inches by $10\frac{1}{2}$ inches approx.) is an ideal size, but if foolscap is used, I recommend that it be typed sideways on a wide carriage typewriter, with one page on each half of the folded sheet.

A typical catalogue entry might read like either of the following examples:

16. Sir Robert de Bures. (?) 1302. Acton, Suffolk.
   A cross-legged figure in mail and surcoat, carrying a large shield of arms; note the embossed design on the knee defences and the broad swordbelt. Considered to be one of the finest military brasses in existence. Length 6 ft. $7\frac{1}{2}$ inches.

If the exhibition is a small or selective one, a fuller entry such as this might be used:

27. Sir John Peryent and wife Joan. 1415. Digswell, Herts.
   The male figure wears full plate armour with Esquire's collar and has the unusual feature of a leopard or panther at his feet. Among several offices he held, he was Pennon bearer to King Richard II, Esquire to Kings Henry IV and V and Master of the Horse to Joan of Navarre (second Queen of Henry IV); he died in 1432.
   His wife Joan displays a unique, plaited head-dress with veil, and wears the Lancastrian 'SS' collar of gold; on the left lapel of her dress is embroidered a white swan (a badge

E   65

of the Bohun family under whom she served); at her feet is a hedgehog, the significance of which is uncertain; she died on April 23, 1415.

Finally, it should be borne in mind that it is not always the most famous brasses which will attract the layman's attention – there are dozens of lesser known examples equally worthy of inclusion. The choice of the exhibits is a personal one – the final success or otherwise of the exhibition as a whole, is very much dependent on the visitors and the impressions they take home with them.

Facsimiles of brasses. (a) MINIATURE. For many years now small facsimilies on metal have been available in selected churches (e.g. Stoke D'Abernon, Surrey; Edlesborough, Bucks.). They have a brass-like colour, with the lines of the original reproduced in black; on a few examples the tinctures of the shields of arms are added, e.g. Sir John D'Abernon. These were first made in 1954 by Mr S. A. Illsley and were sold at the churches concerned for about 30s. 0d. each; the small metal plates on which the brasses are reproduced are mounted on a light wood base, the whole composition measuring 8 × 2 inches. The plates are made by photographing a rubbing, then transferring and etching the image on to the plaque by the normal printer's silk screen process. Any number can then be reproduced and are virtually indestructible (see *Church Times* 4th May, 1956 for further details). These have no connection with the similar mass produced copies now seen in many art and craft shops (usually on copper coloured plates).

(b) FULL-SIZE. A very new discovery which has only just appeared on the market for sale, is full-size reproductions of brasses, in metal, mounted on a wooden base. These are made by a firm called Laurent Designs Ltd., of

Dicker Mill, Hertford, and are in effect exact replicas of the original brass. So accurate are the moulds, that every little dent and flaw in the original metal is reproduced and rubbings can be made from the replicas in the normal way. This could, if necessary, save wear and tear on a damaged original, but would not be practical for rubbings made for historical or research purposes, as not all parts of the brass are necessarily reproduced, usually the figures only.

However, the object in making these replicas is not as substitutes but for decorative purposes in the home, and as such they are more than effective. The first copies had a shiny surface, but this has now been replaced with a matt finish more like the original and many people would be hard put to it to tell one from the other. Mounted on a mahogany base, the whole composition can be hung on the wall. With each replica goes a brief explanatory booklet about the brass, with short notes on brass rubbing added. The price of these very fine facsimilies varies from between about 3 guineas to over £60 for a full-size figure about 5 feet 6 inches high. The example illustrated, which cannot do real justice to the product, is a figure some three feet tall. (*See Pl. 13.*)

(B) *Storage of brass rubbings*

By the time you have collected fifty or more rubbings you are up against the inevitable problem of storage and preservation. One early writer in the *Monumental Brass Society Transactions* (M.B.S. Trans.) Vol. 2 (1894) pp. 103–106, the Rev. H. E. Field, suggested reducing rubbings for record and storage purposes by use of the pantograph. He did agree that this was a very time consuming operation and practicable only for the smaller brasses. Whilst one can see the possibilities of this, especially for decorative work or for line illustrations in a book, one shudders at the thought of the labour involved!

There are three basic methods of storage, and one or two alternatives of dubious merit which I shall discuss below. Always bear in mind that any paper, however good its quality, is vulnerable to natural decay, and much more so if stored in conditions conducive to damp, excessive heat or bacteria. While it is obviously impossible and indeed unnecessary in most cases, to produce ideal conditions in the home, certain basic precautions can be taken. Amongst these may be mentioned the following:

(1) Use a good quality rag-based paper, e.g. detail paper.

(2) Store away from strong natural light, especially if the rubbing is permanently displayed or done on lining paper.

(3) Do not store in a room, cellar or attic liable to dampness.

(4) Do not store in a cupboard or room where the atmosphere is very dry, as this makes the paper brittle and more liable to tear.

(5) Store away from excessive dust, as this not only attracts paper eating bacteria, but, in quantity, makes the edges of the paper grubby and discoloured.

(6) If you mount your rubbings, make sure you use a glue or paste which does not attract or harbour bacteria and/or fungi. Flour and water paste (which has many other advantages) has this tendency, especially if used with lining paper. Mice and silver fish particularly enjoy eating paper backed with this type of paste. The use of adhesives has already been discussed under 'Mounting' (p. 57).

Most of these precautions are not necessary unless you intend your rubbings to be kept permanently, or for a period exceeding about three years.

The three most common methods of storage are:

(a) Rolled and unprotected.

(b) Rolled and protected by a cardboard sleeve.

(c) Flat in folders or drawers.

(a) *Rolled.* The ideal collection is one housed in individual carboard sleeves with covers over each and labelled accurately for easy reference, and placed in specially constructed storage racks like those used for a collection of maps. This is the ideal, but for most people the only space available will be a cupboard, a white wood chest, a large trunk or a suitcase. Cardboard sleeves may be saved for the very best or most treasured rubbings, but they are expensive in quantity whether used to roll the rubbing around, or to place it inside. Your local dress shop may be able to supply you with a few old rolls if their fabrics are wound on them.

Rubbings which are rolled take up a good deal of space in quantity, especially if many large compositions several feet wide are included; they are also difficult to keep in order if proper racks are not available. A large cardboard box in which the rolls can be stored upright is a practical and cheap alternative.

The main asset of rolled rubbings is that little damage or creasing occurs provided the ends are protected; this is especially important if the rubbings are to be photographed, since any creases will spoil the print, as already explained in section 2. of this chapter.

(b) *Folded.* The advantages of having a large collection of rubbings stored flat are self-evident, since they take up less space, can be kept in order fairly easily if labelled clearly and can be transported between large millboards if required. Few homes will possess a large plan chest (as used in drawing offices, chart rooms, etc.) which has six or eight wide shallow drawers where many of the rubbings could be stored unfolded. Even these, however, present practical difficulties when one wishes to look at a rubbing at the bottom of a thick pile, and large sheets of cardboard are necessary at intervals to stop the ends curling up.

Millboards, with tapes attached (like those used by artists for transporting their drawings) offer the most practical solution and can be stored either flat or upright; a list of the contents of each folder can be pasted on to the inside of the top board. The one thing users of this method must watch is that the rubbings do not stick out the sides of the folder as they will soon become dirty or damaged; commercially made folders usually have flaps on the sides to prevent this however.

(C) *Cataloguing and indexing a collection.* (*i*) CATALOGU-ING. The importance of this task cannot be emphasised too strongly, for a collection of rubbings bearing no identity or location, is, historically speaking at any rate, almost useless. Every brass rubber will know the famous examples, but those without inscriptions, coats of arms or other means of recognition will probably never be positively identified later. The type of record you keep may be partly governed by the storage facilities available, but whatever method you choose, make sure that each item has some clearly visible code or reference number. Even if you arrange your collection alphabetically by county or place, this will still be necessary for positive identification.

The most frequently used arrangements are:

(a) Alphabetically by county; then subdivided by place name (e.g. Society of Antiquaries Collection).

(b) Alphabetically by place name; subdivided chronologically or by personal name.

(c) Chronologically.

(d) Grouped by type (e.g. civilian; ecclesiastic, military or a combination of (c) and (d).

Mr Malcolm Norris in his book (*op. cit.*) suggests that for the more advanced student with a large collection, arrangement by styles of engraving might be attempted, but this would need considerable experience. I would not recommend a running serial number or letter unless the collection is very small or specialised (e.g. the late Major H. F. Owen Evans, M.B.E., F.S.A., a well known name in brass rubbing circles, specialised in collecting rubbings of brasses depicting the Holy Trinity). The main advantages of the above methods are that they all lend themselves to easy insertion of new entries.

As an example, let me take one of the groups above and devise a hypothetical collection of rubbings. Method (d) seems to offer the most scope for a suitable classification and sub-division, so I will use this in an illustration. The suggested main headings and subdivisions to be arranged chronologically unless otherwise stated.

Group	Main Class		Subdivisions
(A)	Military (excl. tabard)	e.g. (i)	1270–1310
		(ii)	1310–1350
		(iii)	1350–1410
		(iv)	1410–1480
		(v)	1480–1550
		(vi)	1550–1640
		(vii)	1640–1680

(B) Ecclesiastic	(i) Secular	(a)	Archbishops
		(b)	Bishops
		(c)	Deans
		(d)	Canons
		(e)	Priests
		(f)	Deacons
	(ii) Monastic	(a)	Abbots
		(b)	Priors and sub-priors
		(c)	Monks
		(d)	Abbesses
		(e)	Nuns

(C) Civilian   (i) General

(ii) Professions; e.g. notaries; auditors; teachers

(iii) Legal and civic; e.g. judges; aldermen; mayors

(iv) Merchants; tradesmen; etc.; e.g. masons; woolmen

(v) Royal household; e.g. Yeomen of the Guard; Barons of the Exchequer; cooks

(vi) Female (single figures); e.g. widows

(D) Academic   [Could be subdivided by various degrees, but probably better left chronologically]

(E) Continental   (i) Brasses of foreign workmanship in U.K.

(ii) Abroad (subdivided by country then by place name or period)

(F) Special types   e.g. (i) Shroud and skeleton

(ii) Heart

(iii) Chalice

(iv) Chrysom

(v) Rose

(vi) Cross and bracket

(vii) Heraldic, e.g. achievements of arms with inscriptions only

(G) Tabard brasses

(H) Pictographic   e.g. Margate, Kent (1615) – ship in full sail

                                  Buntingford, Herts. (1620) – preaching a sermon

(K) Miscellaneous   e.g. (i) Inscriptions only

                                    (ii) Brasses placed outside church

(L) Palimpsest brasses

The above table is a suggested outline and is capable of many variations and improvements, and is only offered as an example of the type of classification that might be adopted. A very interesting article by J. P. C. Kent, 'Monumental brasses; a new classification of Military Effigies' in the *Journal of the British Archaeological Association*, Vol. XII. (1949) pp. 70–97, could possibly be used in section (A) above, if the chronological sequence I have indicated were not adopted; mine is based on those suggested by the late Sir James Mann.

(*ii*) INDEXING. For the average collector, it is probably not necessary to construct an index, as most of the rubbings will be familiar enough already. If, however, you have built up a larger collection over a number of years, it is quite easy to forget some of your earliest rubbings when you need examples for display or reference purposes. Not many books of any value can manage without some kind of an index, no more than a large collection of paintings, drawings, etc.

The index is best constructed using stiff cards like those used in library catalogues, or paper slips of about the same dimensions (5 × 3 inches approx.); these could be home-made if necessary. Such a card or sheaf index has the great advantage of being compact and easily added to when required. The cards can be filed by place name; date of brass or by type; if the latter is used, then cross references are an advantage. A typical entry might look like the one below:

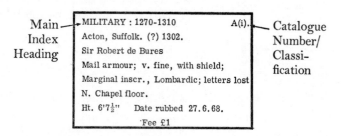

Main Index Heading

MILITARY : 1270-1310   A(i).
Acton, Suffolk. (?) 1302.
Sir Robert de Bures
Mail armour; v. fine, with shield;
Marginal inscr., Lombardic; letters lost
N. Chapel floor.
Ht. 6'7½"   Date rubbed 27.6.68.
Fee £1

Catalogue Number/ Classi- fication

The above can be adapted by altering the main heading to suit the size of the collection, i.e. it could be under 'Acton 'or 'Suffolk: Acton: (?) 1302'. The catalogue or classification number must, however, remain whichever main heading is adopted. The cards can be filed in a commercially made or home-made drawer or box and guide cards bought to divide up the main sections.

Finally, if a much fuller record is required for each rubbing, a loose leaf file is the most practical method as it makes new insertions easy. This can be maintained in the same way as your card index, or if it is in a different order, the card index can bear an identifying symbol or keyword in one of the lower corners to indicate the heading used in the master file. A full entry in the master file might include all or some of the following details:

(a) Catalogue/Index Number.

(b) Location of brass (incl. dedication of church; place; county).

(c) Date rubbed.

(d) Fee paid (if any).

(e) Name(s) of person(s) commemorated.

(f) Date of brass.

(g) Position in church. (e.g. Mural, S. Transept).

(h) General description of brass (incl. details of all accessories, costume, armour, coats of arms, special features).

(i) Transcript of inscription (where existing).

(j) Notes of any indents visible (with measurements)

(k) Vital statistics, i.e. length of figure(s), size of inscription, shields, groups of children, etc.

(l) Size of slab (if in new slab, size of old slab as well, if still existing).

(m) Details of any missing parts, e.g. inscriptions, shields, etc. discovered from search of local archive and book material, e.g. county histories, collections of rubbings, etc.

(n) Any additional biographical/genealogical information not apparent from inscription.

5

How to Find Out About Brasses

Location lists: British Isles. Continental brasses. General books
on brasses, British Isles. Books, periodical articles, about the
brasses in individual counties of the British Isles. Mainland
Europe. Costume. Armour. National collections of brass rubbings
in the U.K. The Monumental Brass Society.

(A) Location lists – British Isles

Printed lists giving the locations of brasses are usually
selective by necessity if they form, as most do, an appendix
to a general work. By far the most comprehensive and
up-to-date list is that compiled by Mr Mill Stephenson
which was based on the earlier one by Haines (see below
for details). The works below in chronological order all
contain lists of varying usefulness and may be considered
as almost comprehensive. Those works which are no longer
in print can usually be seen in, or obtained from, public lending or reference libraries. Fuller bibliographic details of
most of these works are given in section B of this chapter.

(1) MANNING, Charles R. A list of the Monumental
Brasses remaining in England. Arranged according to
Counties. London, F. & J. Rivington. 1846. 94 p.

Arranged alphabetically within each section, details
given include location, identification of brass (i.e. name of
person or type) and date. Useful mainly as early check
list, but not comprehensive and has several typographical
errors in each section.

(2) SIMPSON, Justin. A list of the Sepulchral Brasses of England, alphabetically arranged by counties. Stamford, John Ford. 1857. 108 p.

Similar to (1) above and very scarce. Copy in the British Museum Library and Society of Antiquaries. Any value it might have had is marred by innumerable inaccuracies.

(3) HAINES, Rev. Herbert. *A Manual of Monumental Brasses.* 2 Vols. Part II. A list of the Monumental Brasses of the British Isles. (1861).

Very comprehensive for each county and including book and periodical references for many brasses. Out of print for many years, it has since been superseded by Mill Stephenson's list below, but still has great historical value. Some minor amendments to the list appeared in *Antiquary*, Vol. 5, 1882.

(4) MACKLIN, Rev. Herbert W. *Monumental Brasses.* 1890 *et. seq.* 7th rev. edn. 1953*.

The earlier editions contained county lists, but these were of little value as they were only arranged alphabetically by place within each century, and no further details were given. The 6th edition (1913) was the first to contain expanded County Lists based on Haines', giving details under each location of date and type of brass (i.e. civilian, priest, etc.). This list is repeated in the 7th edition (1953) with a short appendix of corrections (p. 191) resulting from the 1939–45 war.

(5) STEPHENSON, Mill. *A list of Monumental Brasses in the British Isles* (1926). Appendix (1938).

Based on Haines's list, this is the most valuable work currently available. It has been reprinted by the Monu-

---

*This book has been completely re-written by Mr John C. Page-Phillips, and will be published in its new edition shortly.

mental Brass Society and a few copies are still obtainable from the Hon. Publications Custodian of the Society price £5 5s. (£4 4s. to members only). It is hoped to set up a team to revise and up-date the list for each county in the near future (see M.B.S. Newsletter, December 1967).

(6) ASHMOLEAN MUSEUM, OXFORD. Notes on brass rubbings. 5th rev. edn. by H. W. Catling.

This is the first edition to include county lists, based on Mill Stephenson's. Only location and dates are given under each heading, plus sources of information where books or periodical articles exist. There are much fuller lists for churches in the Oxford area, which include details of fees charged for rubbing at each church or college chapel.

CONTINENTAL BRASSES. At the time of writing (April 1968) it was announced that a companion volume to Mill Stephenson's list, (5) above, giving details of continental brasses was to be published by the Monumental Brass Society in the near future. This has been compiled by Dr H. K. Cameron of Cambridge University, Vice President of the Society, and will undoubtedly be of considerable value and interest as no such compilation exists at present.

These are the main sources, but other lists of some interest appear in Malcolm Norris' *Brass Rubbing* (1965) especially useful for its check list of foreign examples; Malcolm Cook's *Discovering Brasses* (1967) which lists the best brasses in the South of England only; and chapters IX (pp. 215–217) and XI (pp. 233–261) of A. C. Bouquet's book *Church Brasses* (1956) which has select lists of palimpsest brasses and indents of brasses, but these are of very limited value only.

Many people, once they have collected a representative

set of brass rubbings, will wish to learn more about each one or about brasses generally. In time this interest will broaden and deepen, and the list of books and periodicals below will, I hope, act as a useful guide to the literature of brasses for those so inclined. Unfortunately, many of those cited are long out of print and can only be obtained from, or seen in, libraries or second-hand bookshops. Those still in print, should you wish to buy them, have the publication price given after the publisher's name; prices given are those in force at the time of writing (April 1968) and do not take into account any subsequent increases following reprinting, etc. The list is arranged approximately in order of publication.

(B) General works – English brasses

(1) BOUTELL Rev. Charles. *Monumental Brasses and Slabs.* (G. Bell. 1947. xv, 235 p. illus.)

A very thorough and interesting pioneer work on which many subsequent books were based. Arising from a series of talks given by the author in 1846, it deals with each class of brass (i.e. civilian, military, etc.) and has a good section on Flemish brasses (pp. 165–169). Notes on brass rubbing techniques show how very little they have changed in 120 years. There are appendices listing the finest brasses within each class and contemporary suppliers of brass rubbing materials. Many good illustrations.

(2) BOUTELL, Rev. Charles. *Monumental Brasses of England, a Series of Engravings on Wood.* (G. Bell and others. 1849. 53 p. +152 plates).

Engravings drawn from rubbings, with some examples 'restored' by the artists. Brief historical notes are given on each plate at the beginning of the book.

(3) OXFORD ARCHITECTURAL SOCIETY. *A Manual for the*

study of Monumental Brasses. ed. H. Haines. (Parker. 1848. *cxiv*, 227 p. illus.)

A fore-runner of Haines' book below, the format and style of this work is identical in places to Haines' first volume. Now largely of historical value only, it is an interesting pioneer work in the field. Includes topographical list of 450 rubbings possessed by the Society.

(4) WALLER, John G. and WALLER, Lionel A. B. *A series of Monumental Brasses from the 13th to the 16th Century.* Pts. 1–10 [usually bound in one volume]. (J. B. Nichols & Sons. 1842–64).

Sixty very fine, tinted plates, some in colour, and several of brasses since lost or mutilated. Each brass is described in some detail and while this rare and valuable work is not essential for the beginner, it is well worth seeing should the opportunity arise.

(5) HAINES, Rev. Herbert. *A Manual of Monumental Brasses.* Pts. I and II. (Parker. 1861. Vol. I Text, 263 p. Vol. II County Lists, 286 p.)

Still regarded by many authorities as the standard work on brasses despite its age. Unfortunately long out of print, even second-hand copies are rare. Not essential to the beginner, but for the person interested in the history and development of brasses an invaluable reference book. The chapter on the origin of brasses needs using with care however, in the light of more recent research. The county lists already referred to above are of great historical value and a remarkable compilation for their time.

(6) CAMBRIDGE University Association of Brass Collectors, Transactions.

Vol. I Nos. 1–10, 1887–91.

Vol. II Pts. I & II, Nos. 11 and 12, Sept. 1892 and August 1893.

Plate 11. Sir John Poyle and wife Elizabeth. 1424. Hampton-Poyle, Oxfordshire. Another 'rubbing' on aluminium foil which, in the female figure and inscription especially, exhibits a marked resemblance to the texture and appearance of the original brass. It also illustrates the considerable problems of lighting such 'rubbings' for photographing. (*See Chapter 4.*) Photo: Aluminium Federation

Plate 12. Sir John Seyntmour and wife Elizabeth. 1485. Beckington, Somerset. This screen print was produced by the photographic method outlined in Chapter 4, and illustrates clearly how closely it resembles the original rubbing. This print is on paper, but it could be made on cloth equally well. (*See Chapter 4.*) Photo: Henry W. Gray.
Original rubbing and screen print by Julia Crallan

From Vol. II Pt. III, No. 13 this became the present
MONUMENTAL BRASS SOCIETY TRANSACTIONS (New
Series No. 1) 1st January, 1894.

Invaluable as a reference source for articles on brasses
in individual counties and countries; notes and news of new
discoveries, e.g. palimpsest brasses, indents; general and
specialised articles on the history of brasses; detailed
articles on individual brasses or the brasses of a particular
church. Together with the Portfolio of the Monumental
Brass Society, containing large reproductions of brasses
and indents of special interest (first issued in 1894) these
publications are essential to any serious student as well as
to the interested beginner. The current issues of the
Transactions and Portfolio are published every few years
for members of the Society.

(7) (a) OXFORD *Journal of Monumental Brasses.*
Vol. I 1897–99.
Vol. II Pts. 1 & 2, 1900, Part 3, 1912. No more
published.
(b) OXFORD *Portfolio of Monumental Brasses.*(1898
to date).

Oxford University Archaeological Society (formerly published by Oxford University Brass-rubbing Society).

A varied collection of general articles on the history of
brasses, plus notes on new discoveries, with special
reference to those in the Oxford area. The Portfolio is
similar to that of the M.B.S. above.

(8) MACKLIN, Rev. Herbert W. *Monumental Brasses.*
7th rev. edn. with new preface by Sir Charles Oman.
(Allen & Unwin. 16s. 0d. 1953, repr. 1966, 196 p. illus.)
First published in 1890, this little book is still a useful
introduction for the beginner, provided the notes in the
new preface are heeded. The section classifying military

brasses must be read with care. The county lists in the new edition are a valuable addition (*cf. footnote p. 77*).

(9) MACKLIN, Rev. Herbert W. *The Brasses of England.* (Methuen [Antiquaries Books]. 1907. 307 p. illus.).

An excellent handbook now regrettably long out of print, but dealing in great detail with every aspect and type of brass. Many examples are quoted and the work is well illustrated. As with his other book the section on military brasses should be read with care as some of the terminology is not correct. Macklin was a President of the M.B.S. and Rector of Houghton Regis in Bedfordshire.

(10) SUFFLING, Ernest R. *English Church Brasses from the 13th to the 17th Century.* (L. Upcott Gill. 1910. 456 p. 237 illus.)

The first of several books similar to that of Macklin's above (No. 9) and useful mainly for its many illustrations. The county lists at the end are too full of errors to be of much value.

(11) WARD, J. S. M. *Brasses.* (Cambridge U.P. 1912. 159 p. illus.).

A small handbook arranged mainly by historical periods, and a useful introduction for anyone able to buy or borrow a copy. Pages 112–147 have appendices listing examples of various types of brasses, e.g. civilian, shroud, heart. The index is arranged topographically.

(12) BEAUMONT, Edward T. *Ancient Memorial Brasses.* (Oxford U.P. 1913. 197 p. 78 illus.)

Based very much on Macklin's book (No. 9 above) this now almost forgotten work is still worth reading for its general detail on costume, armour, etc., but adds little new to the subject. Well illustrated.

(13) VICTORIA & ALBERT MUSEUM. *A list of rubbings of brasses classified and arranged in chronological order.*

(H.M.S.O. 1915. illus. 2nd edn., pub. by Board of Education, 1929).

Contains many good photographs of rubbings in the Museum's collection, though some of the larger brasses are so reduced in size as to make them indistinct. The lists are useful as a guide to what are ostensibly the best brasses in each class, but no indication of the condition is given, nor of any missing parts; the details given are based on Haine's list. There are name and place indexes, and a list of foreign brasses and incised slabs is also included (pp. 74–82 of first edition.).

(14) CLAYTON, Rev. H. J. *The Ornaments of the Ministers as shown on English Monumental Brasses.* Alcuin Club Collections XXII. (A. R. Mowbray. 1919. 190 p. illus.)

A specialised treatise illustrating the development of ecclesiastical vestments as seen on brasses. Historical introduction followed by eighty-three plates with descriptive text. Not too technical to be understood by the average enthusiast.

(15) GAWTHORP, Walter E. *The Brasses of Our Homeland Churches.* (Homeland Assn. Ltd. [Pocket Books No. 14] 1923. 130 p. illus.)

Despite its small format a very useful little book full of good illustrations. Has interesting chapters on engraving of brasses, applying colours to brasses, merchants marks and making and storing rubbings. A much neglected little book now long out of print. As with all the early books the classification and some of the terminology connected with armour must be used with care.

(16) BOUQUET, Rev. A. C. *Church brasses; British and Continental, with some notes on Incised Stone Slabs and indents.* (Batsford. 1956. 284 p. illus.)

The first of the post 1939–45 books on brasses, but one regrettably marred by numerous inaccuracies. The illustrations are plentiful, but vary in quality; there is a coloured frontispiece taken from Cotman's book below (p. 94). The lists of indents (*op. cit.*) and palimpsests (pp. 215–217) are of very limited use as few dates are given. A book to be used with great care.

(17) MANN, Sir James G. *Monumental Brasses.* (Penguin Books. 5s. 0d. 1957. 72 p. illus.)

An extremely well produced little book with very good illustrations. Particularly useful for its detail of armour, correcting many mistakes by earlier writers on brasses on the terminology of arms and armour. The forty pages of text include a short historical introduction, bibliography and index.

(18) FRANKLYN, Julian. *Brasses.* (Arco Publications. 42s. 0d. 1964. 156 p. illus.)

One of the first books to break with the traditional method of describing the development and history of brasses. It has two useful glossaries on armour and ecclesiastical vestments, as well as a unique guide to reading black letter inscriptions, plus appendices of Anglo-Norman, medieval Latin and middle-English words found on brasses. The illustrations are few but good. There is no section on brass rubbing as the author disapproves of the practice 'for fun'. Despite its rather high cost, it is well worth buying should the occasion arise.

(19) ASHMOLEAN MUSEUM, OXFORD. *Notes on Brass Rubbing* . . . 5th rev. edn. by H. W. Catling. (The Museum. 2s. 6d. 1965. 70 p. paper covers).

For the beginner probably the best short introduction I can recommend. It has plenty of useful references, a bibliography and in its present edition, county lists of brasses based on those of Mill Stephenson. The section on brass rubbing is necessarily concise, but all the basic information is there. Additional information includes a glossary of terms used in costume and armour and notes on collections of rubbings of national importance. Available also through booksellers or from Phillips & Page Ltd. (*op. cit.*).

(20) NORRIS, Malcolm. *Brass Rubbing*. (Studio Vista. 35s. 0d. 1965. 112 p. illus.).

Despite its somewhat misleading title, this is certainly the best general book to be written since Macklin's in 1907. Concise, accurate, copiously illustrated, it contains more on the history and development of brasses than on actual brass rubbing as the title suggests (17 out of the 112 pages). A certain amount of knowledge of the subject is an advantage to fully appreciate this work. Amongst its special features are a 'narrative' bibliography, a brief list of the best brasses in Great Britain and Europe, and excellent sections on the manufacture of brasses and on foreign brasses of which Mr Norris and others have made a special study. The index is the only poor feature.

(21) COOK, Malcolm. *Discovering brasses: a Guide to Monumental Brasses*. (Shire Publications, Gubblecote, Tring, Herts. 3s. 6d. paper back. 1967. 48 p.)

A pocket-sized book strictly for the beginner, but containing most of the basic facts in a concise and readable form. The traditional pattern of describing brasses by type is followed. There are short sections on brass rubbing and a select list of 'Outstanding brasses in Southern England'. Apart from the two line drawings at the end, the illustrations are adequate within the limits imposed on them by the paper, though some lack clarity.

(22) CHAMBERS' ENCYCLOPAEDIA. rev. edn. 1967. Vol. II
Brasses, Monumental by Sir James G. Mann. pp. 494–496.

A very concise and useful introduction by an eminent
authority (see 17 above); especially helpful on general
details of armour. There is a short bibliography but
regrettably only one illustration.

(23) BOUQUET, Rev. A. C. and WARING, Michael.
European Brasses. (Batsford. £6 6s. 1967. 79 p. 32 plates.)

A very large volume (21 by 14¼ inches) consisting of a
short historical introduction and 32 very fine black and
white illustrations of brasses from Britain and the continent of Europe. Each plate has accompanying text
opposite of varying usefulness and length, but far too many
have text not strictly related to the example illustrated –
in some cases it seems almost superfluous. The illustrations
themselves are a great credit to the publisher, but one
doubts the real value of such a work. It is the first work of
this size to be produced on this scale since Creeny's in
1884 (c.f. below), though many of the plates contained in
the latter are reproduced again here. Strictly a book for
the ardent enthusiast or collector, but interesting as an
illustration of the splendour of some of the great Flemish
brasses in particular. Fifteen English and seventeen continental brasses are illustrated.

(24) TRIVICK, Henry. *The Craft and Design of Monumental Brasses.* (John Baker. £9 9s. 1968.) (Not published at time of writing – announced in publisher's
catalogue, Spring 1968.)

BOOKS, ARTICLES, ETC. ON INDIVIDUAL COUNTIES IN THE
BRITISH ISLES (other than those above)

Most of the works cited below are only available in
libraries, but for those interested enough to want to search

further into the history of the brasses in their own area, this list will act as a useful guide to the principal sources of information. Nearly all of them can be seen at the Society of Antiquaries in London should they not be readily available elsewhere, but you should make every effort to obtain them locally before approaching the Society itself (see note on p. 104). No attempt has been made to assess each work and its inclusion does not mean that it is necessarily recommended.

BEDFORDSHIRE

(1) FISHER, Thomas. *Collections historical, genealogical and topographical for Bedfordshire.* (Nichols & Sons. 1812–36. Supplementary volume 1828.)

Contains many excellent drawings of brasses, many now lost or damaged. An important basic source.

(2) SANDERSON, H. K. St J. *The Brasses of Bedfordshire.* M.B.S. Trans. Vol. 2 1893–96. pp. 33–45, 74–90, 117–133, 153–174, 193–213, 275–291. Vol. 3 1897 pp. 31–41. illus.

(3) ISHERWOOD, Grace. *Monumental Brasses in the Bedfordshire Churches.* illus. by Kitty Isherwood. (Elliot Stock. 1906. 68 p.)

A shorter article appears in (a) *The Bedfordshire Architectual and Archaeological Society Papers*, 1883, p. 77 (Addington, Rev. H. *The Brasses of Bedfordshire*) and (b) Archaeological J, XL(159) 1883. (A reprint of the same article.)

BERKSHIRE

MORLEY, Henry T. *Monumental Brasses of Berkshire* (*fourteenth to seventeenth century*). (Reading: The Electric Press. 1924. 262 p. illus. from author's own rubbings.)

CAMBRIDGESHIRE

(1) NEALE, J. M. (*editor*). *Illustrations of Monumental Brasses in Cambridge* (Camb. Camden Soc. 1840–46. 24 plates).

(2) CAVE, C. J. P., CHARLTON, O. J. and MACALISTER, R.A.S. *compilers. The Brasses of Cambridgeshire.*

M.B.S. Trans. Vol. 2 (1893–96) pp. 174–179, 237–275, 307–314. illus.

M.B.S. Trans. Vol. 3 (1897–99) pp. 2–30, 88. illus.

M.B.S. Trans. Vol. 4 (1900–03) pp. 60–78, 176. illus.

M.B.S. Trans. Vol. 5 (1904) pp. 8–16, 39–48. illus.

Unfortunately the series was not completed.

(3) ROYAL COMMISSION ON HISTORICAL MONUMENTS. *City of Cambridge.* Pts. 1 and 2 . (H.M.S.O. £5 5s. set. 1959).

Includes photographs of some of the brasses *in situ* with brief details of each one cited.

(4) CAMBRIDGE CITY LIBRARIES. *Monumental Brasses in Cambridgeshire and the Isle of Ely.* 3rd revised edn. 2s. 6d. May, 1968.

Cambridge City Libraries, Guildhall, Cambridge. 28 p. bibliog. typescript.

A completely revised edition arranged alphabetically, and including notes on charges for rubbings; plus indexes of names, a chronological list of figure brasses and a short list of sources of illustrations. Figure brasses only are listed throughout.

CHESHIRE

(1) THORNLEY, James L. *Monumental Brasses of Lancashire and Cheshire.* (Hull: William Andrews, The Hull Press; London: Simpkin Marshall. 1893. 322 p. illus.)

Deals with each county in chronological order. Includes 22 Lancashire and 5 Cheshire churches.

(2) BUTTERWORTH, Lionel M. Angus. *Monumental Brasses of Cheshire*. Trans. Lancs. & Cheshire Antiquarian Soc. Vol. LV (1940) pp. 81–106. illus.

CORNWALL

DUNKIN, Edwin H. W. *Monumental Brasses of Cornwall*. (Spottiswoode & Co. 1882. 107 p. 62 plates.)

CUMBERLAND

BOWER, Rev. Canon Richard. *Brasses in the Diocese of Carlisle*. (Kendal, Westmorland; T. Wilson. 1894. *Pamphlet*.) Reprinted from Trans, Cumberland & Westmorland Antiquarian and Archaeological Soc. Vol. XIII, 1894. pp. 142–151. illus.

DERBYSHIRE

FIELD, Rev. H. Eardley. *Monumental Brasses of Derbyshire* (in eight parts). M.B.S. Trans. Vol. 3 (1897–99) pp. 194–196, 209–215. Vol. 5 (1904) pp. 1–7, 29–39, 101–111, 129–138, 171–180, 380–389. illus.

DEVONSHIRE

(1) CRABBE, William R. *An account of the Monumental Brasses remaining in the Churches of the County of Devon, with two appendices*. (Exeter: William Pollard. 1859. illus.)

Reprinted from four part article in Trans. of the Exeter Diocesan Archaeological Society.

(2) ROGERS, William H. H. *The Ancient Sepulchral Effigies and Monumental and Memorial Sculpture of Devonshire*. (Pub. in Exeter, 1877.) (See also note p. 109.)

DORSET

PRIDEAUX, William de Courcey. *Ancient Memorial Brasses*

of Dorset (11 parts). Proc. Dorset Natural Hist. & Antiquarian Field Club. Vol. XXIII (1902) p. 195 to Vol. XXXVII (1907) p. 105 and Vol. XL (1920). illus.

DURHAM

See Northumberland.

ESSEX

(1) CHANCELLOR, Frederick. *Ancient Sepulchral Monuments of Essex.* (Printed for the author. 1890. 418 p. illus.)

(2) CHRISTY, Miller and PORTEOUS, W. W. *Some interesting Essex Brasses* (in 12 parts). Trans. Essex Archaeol. Soc. Vol. VI (1897) – Vol. XIII (1915). illus.

(3) CHRISTY, Miller and others. *Monumental Brasses of Essex.* Pt. I (1948). Pat. II (1951). Still in progress. illus.

(4) *Ditto.* On some interesting brasses in Essex. Reliquary & Illustrated Archaeologist (New Series) Vol. 5 (1899) pp. 9–21. illus.

(5) CAMBRIDGE UNIVERSITY. Monumental Brass Society. *The Monumental Brasses of Essex,* edited by R. H. D'Elboux (Ashford. 1948).

GLOUCESTERSHIRE

DAVIS, Cecil T. *Monumental Brasses of Gloucestershire.* (Phillimore & Co. 1899. 230 p. illus.)

First issued as suppt. to quarterly parts of Gloucestershire Notes & Queries, Vols. 5, 6 & 7. (1894–99).

Arranged largely in chronological order; includes list of lost brasses.

HAMPSHIRE

CAVE, C. J. P. *List of Hampshire Brasses.*

M.B.S. Trans. Vol. 5 (1904–09) pp. 247–291, 295–325, 343-371.

Vol. 6 (1910–13) pp. 1–39, 121–157. well illus.

HEREFORDSHIRE

(1) HAINES, Rev. Herbert. *Monumental Brasses in the Cathedral and County of Hereford.* J. British Archaeol. Assn. Vol. XXVII (1871) pp. 85, 198, 541.

(2) DAVIS, Cecil T. *Monumental Brasses of Hereford and Worcestershire* (1885. 24 p. illus.) (Repr. from Trans. Birmingham & Midland Institute, 1884–5, p. 62 *et seq.*)

(3) INGRAM, A. J. Winnington, *Monumental Brasses in Hereford Cathedral* . . . a lecture given . . . 27th January, 1955. (Hereford. 1956. 16 p. illus.)

HERTFORDSHIRE

(1) ANDREWS, William F. *Memorial brasses in Hertford-shire Churches.* 2nd edn. (Elliot Stock. 1903. 172 p.)

First published in smaller edition, but again without illustrations, 1886.

(2) ANDREWS, Herbert C. *Sidelights on Brasses in Hertfordshire Churches.* East Herts Archaeol. Soc. Trans. Vol. VIII, Pt. 2 1930–31 (pub. 1933). – Vol. XIII, Pt. 2. 1952–54 (1955); Albury-Eastwick. Following the death of Mr. Andrews the series was continued from Vol. XIV, Pt. 1. 1955–57 (1959), Essendon onwards, by Richard J. Busby, and is still in progress.*

*From 1968 this journal will be re-named *Hertfordshire Archaeology* and is the first joint publication of the East Herts Archaeological Society and the St Albans Architectural & Archaeological Society.

HUNTINGDONSHIRE

(1) FRENCH, Rev. Valpy. *The Brasses of Huntingdonshire.* Antiquary, Vol. IV, 1881, pp. 44, 115.

(2) MACKLIN, Rev. Herbert W. *Brasses of Huntingdonshire.* M.B.S. Trans. Vol. 3, Pts. 3 & 4. (1898–99) pp. 144–160, 167–182. illus.

ISLE OF WIGHT

(1) STONE, Percy G. *Architectural Antiquaries of the Isle of Wight from the eleventh to the seventeenth centuries inclusive.* 4 Pts. in 2 vols. (The author. 1891).

Records brasses at Arreton, Calbourne, Freshwater, Kingston and Shorwell only.

(2) LEWIS, R. M. W. (comp.) *Complete List of the Brasses of the Isle of Wight.* Trans. Camb. Univ. Assn. Brass Collectors, Vol. II Pt. I (1892) pp. 2–6.

KENT

(1) BELCHER, William D. *Kentish Brasses.* 2 Vols.

Vol. I Sprague & Co. 1888. 119 p. incl. 109 pages of plates.

Vol. II. Sprague & Co. 1905. illus.

(2) FISHER, Thomas. (*del.*) *Drawings of Brasses in some Kentish Churches*, edited by Ralph Griffin. (John Bale, Sons & Danielson. 1913. 12 plates.)

(3) GRIFFIN, Ralph. *Kentish Items.* (1955). (Repr. from a series of articles in the M.B.S. Trans. and bound into one volume. Copy at Society of Antiquaries Library.)

(4) GRIFFIN, Ralph and STEPHENSON, Mill. *A List of Monumental Brasses remaining in the County of Kent 1922; with notes of some lost examples.* (Headley Bros. 1923. 245 p. 32 plates.)

(5) MONUMENTAL BRASS SOCIETY. *Some illustrations of*

Monumental Brasses and Indents in Kent. (Headley Bros. for M.B.S. 1946. 47 pages of plates reprinted from articles by Ralph Griffin in the M.B.S. Trans.)

LANCASHIRE
See Cheshire.

LINCOLNSHIRE
(1) JEANS, Rev. George E. *A List of the Existing Sepulchral Brasses in Lincolnshire.* (Horncastle. 1895. 116 p. No illus. Repr. from Lincs. Notes & Queries.)

(2) LINCOLN CATHEDRAL. *Lost Brasses and Indents.* M.B.S. Trans. Vol. 2 (1893–96) pp. 326; Vol. 3. (1897–99) pp. 67, 119. Plan; illus. (150 listed).

LONDON
(1) BELOE, Edward M. *A series of photo-lithographs of Monumental Brasses in Westminster Abbey . . .* (1896).

(2) ROYAL COMMISSION ON HISTORICAL MONUMENTS. London, Vol. I. *Westminster Abbey.* (H.M.S.O. 1924. 142 p. Plates 182–184 show brasses *in situ.*) Includes many refs. to brasses and indents.

(3) ROYAL COMMISSION ON HISTORICAL MONUMENTS. London, Vol. II. *West London.* (H.M.S.O. 1925. 194 p.)

(4) MISSELBROOK, C. G. *The Monumental Brasses of All Hallows by the Tower.* (All Hallows Porchroom, Byward Street, E.C.3. 1953. 21 p. illus.)

MIDDLESEX
CAMERON, Dr. H. K. *The Brasses of Middlesex.* Trans. London & Middx. Archaeol. Soc. (New Series). Vol. X, Pt. 3. 1951 – still in progress. illus.

NORFOLK

(1) COTMAN, John Sell. *Engravings of Sepulchral Brasses in Norfolk and Suffolk.* 2nd edn. with additional plates and notes . . . (Henry Bohn. 2 vols. 1839).

Vol. I. *xvi*, 67 p. + 81 plates. Coloured frontispiece.

Vol. II. 31 p. + 47 plates. Coloured frontispiece.

With those of Thomas Fisher (see Bedfordshire and Kent) some of the finest drawings of brasses ever made, and a pioneer work in the field.

(2) FARRER, Rev. Edmund. *A List of the Monumental Brasses remaining in the County of Norfolk.* (Norwich; Goose & Son. 1890. 128 p. some editions only illus.) Lists 287 figure brasses and 773 inscriptions only in 351 churches. A list of corrections to the above appears in the Trans. Camb. Univ. Assn. Brass Collectors. Vol. I. (1891) p. 14.

(3) BELOE, Edward M. *A series of photo-lithographs of Monumental Brasses in Norfolk.* (1890–91. 25 plates.)

NORTHAMPTONSHIRE

(1) HARTSTHORNE, Rev. Charles H. *An endeavour to classify the sepulchral remains of Northamptonshire* (Cambridge; Pitt Press: Oxford; Parker. 1840. 58 p. illus.)

Deals mainly with ecclesiastical and military brasses.

(2) HUDSON, Franklin. *Brasses of Northamptonshire.* (1853. 90 illus. in bronze colouring.)

(3) BUSHNELL, G. S. and RUCK, G. E. A. *Monumental Brasses of Northamptonshire.* (Northants Archit. & Archaeol. Soc. Reports & Papers Vol. 53 (1947)).

(4) GREENHILL, F. A. *Some additions to the Northamptonshire List* (i). M.B.S. Trans. Vol 9. Pt. V. (1955) p. 272. Still in progress. illus.

NORTHUMBERLAND

(1) WALLER, J. G. *Notes on some brasses in the Counties of Northumberland and Durham.*

(2) Archaeologia Aeliana. Vol. XV. (1892) pp. 76–88, 207, 311. illus. Article: The monumental brasses of Northumberland and Durham.

NOTTINGHAMSHIRE

(1) BRISCOE, John P. and FIELD, Rev. H. Eardley. *Monumental Brasses of Nottinghamshire.* Pt. I. (1904. 40 p. illus.) No further parts published.

(2) THORNTON SOCIETY, Transactions. Vols. XIII, p. 15; XIV, p. 5; XVI, p. 165 and mainly XVII, p. 127–131. illus.

OXFORDSHIRE

(1) OXFORD *Journal of Monumental Brasses.* Vols. 1–3. 1897–1912. (*c.f.* general list No. 7 (a).)

(2) GUNTHER, R. T. *Brasses in the Chapel of Magdalen College.* (Pamphlet obtainable from The Old Library, Magdalen College, Oxford. Price 3s. 6d.)

(3) ROYAL COMMISSION ON HISTORICAL MONUMENTS. *City of Oxford.* (H.M.S.O. £5 5s. 1939. Repr. 1966. 244 p.)

Brief details of all brasses and indents are given for every College chapel and church in the City.

SHROPSHIRE

STEPHENSON, Mill. *Monumental Brasses in Shropshire.* (March; Harris & Sons. 1895. 56 p. illus.) Repr. from Archaeol. J. Vol. LII (1895) pp. 47–102. The same article was also published in the Transactions Shropshire Archaeol. Soc. (2nd series) Vol. VII. (1895). pp. 384–440.

SOMERSET

CONNOR, Arthur B. *Monumental Brasses in Somerset.*
Proc. of the Somersetshire Archaeol. & Nat. Hist. Soc. Vol.
LXXVII (1931) in 22 parts until Vol. XCVIII (1955).
illus. Short Index to series Vol. CIII (1958–59) pp. 72–75.
(under places and families).

STAFFORDSHIRE

MASEFIELD, Charles. *Monumental Brasses of Staffordshire.* Trans. North Staffs. Field Club. Vol. XLVII (1912–
13) pp. 157–173. illus. Postscript: Vol. XLIX (1914–15)
pp. 99–102.

SUFFOLK

(1) COTMAN, John Sell. *Suffolk Brasses* . . . 38 plates.
(Henry Bohn. 1838.) See also under Norfolk.

(2) BRITISH MUSEUM Additional MS. 32483–4. Complete collection of rubbings of Suffolk brasses made in
nineteenth century by David E. Davy, Suffolk historian.
(See Mill Stephenson's List p. 446.)

(3) FARRER, Rev. Edmund. *A List of Monumental
Brasses remaining in the County of Suffolk.* (Norwich;
Goose Ltd., 1903. 93 p. illus.)

Includes brief historical introduction on history of
brasses.

SURREY

(1) STEPHENSON, Mill. M.B.S. Trans. Vol. 6. (1910–14)
pp. 257–295, 329–352, 377– 398. illus.

(2) SURREY ARCHAEOL. COLLECTIONS. Vol. XXV. (1912)
to Vol. XXXIII. (1920) and Vol. XL. (1932) pp. 107–
116. illus.

(3) A list of Papers on Monumental Brasses in the

Plate 13.
The most popular of a series of full size facsimiles of brasses made by an enterprising British firm, Laurent Designs Ltd of Hertford (see p. *66* for details). Made in metal closely resembling the original brass and mounted on a hardwood base, the moulds from which these facsimiles are cast are so accurate that every detail, good or bad, of the original is reproduced. These copies are proving very popular with American visitors to Britain. (*See Chapter 4.*) Photo: Laurent Designs Ltd

Plate 14.
Roger Thornton
and wife. 1429.
All Saints',
Newcastle-on-Tyne.
This is the finest
civilian brass in the
North of England and
is of Flemish design.
Unlike English brasses
most continental
examples have the
background and
surrounding areas
filled in with diaper
work, allegorical
designs, to form one
solid area of metal.
Rubbing brasses of
this type takes many
hours of hard work.
(*See Chapter 4.*)

'Surrey Archaeological Collections'. Vols. I–XII. (1887–99). M.B.S. Trans. Vol. 3, Pt. 2. (1897–99) pp. 57–60, 206–8.

SUSSEX

(1) WOODMAN, T. C. *The Sussex Brasses*. Pts. I & II in one volume. (Hove; Emery & Son. 1903. 114 p. illus.) Reprinted from the *Hove Gazette.* Some of illus. very poor; no index.

(2) MACKLIN, Rev. Herbert W. *Sussex Brasses*. Contained in: *Memorials of Old Sussex*. pp. 127–153. (Allen & Unwin. 1909.)

(3) MOSSE, H. R. *Monumental Effigies of Sussex*. (1250–1650). Cover title *Sussex Brasses and Effigies*. 2nd edn. 1933. 241 p.

(4) HOUSTON, C. E. D. Davidson. *Sussex Monumental Brasses*. Sussex Archaeol. Coll. Vols. LXXVI to LXXX (1935–39).

Pt. I   Amberley – Buxted (pp. 46–114) illus.

Pt. II   Chichester Cathedral – Friston (pp. 130–194) illus.

Pt. III Goring – North Mundham (pp. 63–125) illus.

Pt. IV Ninfield – Stanmer (pp. 73–130) illus.

Pt. V   Singleton – West Wittering (pp. 93–147). illus.

(5) D'ELBOUX, Raymond Herbert. *Sussex Monumental Brasses*. Surrey Archaeol. Coll. Vol. LXXXVI. (1947).

WARWICKSHIRE

(1) WILLIAMS, Charles. A few notes on monumental brasses, with a catalogue of those existing in Warwickshire. Birmingham & Midland Institute Trans. (Archaeological Section). 1884–85, pp. 16–51.

(2) BADGER, Rev. Edward W. *The Monumental Brasses*

of *Warwickshire. Accurately transcribed, with Translations and Descriptive Notes.* (Birmingham; Cornish Bros. 1895. 66 p.) No illustrations; only 100 copies printed.

WESTMORLAND
See Cumberland.

WILTSHIRE
KITE, Edward. *The Monumental Brasses of Wiltshire* . . . (Printed for the author and sold by John Henry and James Parker. 1860. 111 p. + 32 plates.)

Limited edition of 250 copies. Includes good illus. of brass of Bishop Hallam in Constance Cathedral, West Germany.

WORCESTERSHIRE
(1) DAVIS, Cecil T. *Monumental Brasses of Herefordshire and Worcestershire.* (1885. 24 p. illus.) Repr. from Trans. Birmingham & Midland Institute 1884–85. p. 62 *et seq.*

(2) THACKER, Francis James and others. *Monumental Brasses of Worcestershire.* Trans. Worcestershire Archaeol. Soc. Vols. III (1927) to XVI (1940).

Vol. III. Pt. I. (1925–26) Alvechurch – Bromsgrove. pp. 107–127.

Vol. IV. Pt. II. (1926–27) Bushley – Fladbury. pp. 129–156.

Vol. XI. Pt. III. (1934–35) Halesowen – Kidderminster. pp. 139–143.

Vol. XV. Pt. IV. (1938–39) Lindridge – Ripple. pp. 1–9.

Vol. XVI. Pt. II. (1939–40) Spetchley – Yardley. pp. 1–13.

From the 1934 issue articles by E. A. B. Barnard and J. F. Parker.

YORKSHIRE

(1) FAIRBANK, F. R. *Ancient Memorial Brasses remaining in the old Deanery of Doncaster.* Yorks. Archaeol. J. Vol. XI. (1891) pp. 71–92. illus.

(2) STEPHENSON, Mill. *The Monumental Brasses of Yorkshire.* Yorkshire Archaeol. J. Vols XII–XXIV (1893–1918). Additions and corrections. Vols. XX–XXIV.

SCOTLAND

(A) Edinburgh (St Giles)

Proc. Soc. of Antiquaries of Scotland, Vol. I. p. 146. illus.

(B) Aberdeen (St Nicholas)

(1) *Proc. Soc. of Antiquaries of Scotland*, Vol. XI. pp. 456–457. illus.

(2) DAVIS, Cecil T. *Monumental Brasses in the Old or West Church, Aberdeen.* (Harrison & Sons. 1894.) Repr. from Archaeol. Journal.

(3) GREENHILL, F. A. *Scottish Notes III.* Aberdeen (St Nicholas). M.B.S. Trans. Vol. IX. Pt. 2 (1952) pp. 92–95.

(C) Ormiston, East Lothian.

Proc. Soc. of Antiquaries of Scotland, Vol. IV. p. 226. illus.

WALES

Coverage incomplete, but most noted in various issues of the Archaeologia Cambrensis, especially the 1st and 5th series. A good article on the series of brasses at Llanwrest, Denbighshire is in Antiquary Vol. XL, pp. 275–277, 338–339 and Vol. XLI, p. 424.

IRELAND

(1) MACKLIN, Herbert W. *St Patrick's Cathedral Dublin.* Camb. Univ. Assn. of Brass Collectors, Trans. Vol. I. No. 10. Sept. 1891. p. 20–23.

(2) Lancs. & Cheshire Antiquarian Soc. Trans. Vol. XI. 1893 (pub. 1894) pp. 34–51. RENAUD, Frank. *Monumental brasses of Sir Edward Fitton and Dean Robert Sutton in St Patrick's, Dublin.*

THE CONTINENT OF EUROPE

(1) CREENY, Rev. W. F. *A Book of Facsimiles of Monumental Brasses on the Continent of Europe.* (Privately printed. 1884. 73 p. illus.)

Now long out of print, but still the standard work despite its now being out of date. Slightly larger in size than A. C. Bouquet's recent book (cf. above) it has eighty-two separate plates of excellent quality, each with good accompanying text. Fifteen of the plates in Creeny are reproduced again by Bouquet. Many of the brasses shown have since been destroyed or mutilated during the two world wars; others are now in Museums. A short pamphlet supplementing Creeny's remarkable book was published as a 'Report of the Peterborough Archaeological Society' in 1932, but offers little new information.

(2) Apart from the information in Mr Norris' book, the best and most recent work in this field is a series of articles compiled under the editorship of Mr F. A. Greenhill and Dr J. Belonje in the Transactions of the Monumental Brass Society and still in progress. The first in the series is in the M.B.S. Trans. Vol. 9. Pt. 5 (1955) pp. 213–220. Dealing with Germany and the Low Countries, these are detailed, well illustrated and embody all the most recent research and discoveries. Other articles by Malcolm Norris, Dr H. K. Cameron, the late R. H. Pearson and the late Major H. F. Owen Evans are also of value. A particularly interesting article on the centres for, and development of, engraving brasses in Germany by Mr M. W. Norris is

'The Schools of Brasses in Germany' (J. Brit. Archaeol. Assn. (3rd series). Vol. XIX (1958). pp. 34–52). This has several illustrations and is supplemented by the information in his book 'Brass Rubbing' already referred to. A new list of Continental brasses being compiled by Dr H. K. Cameron has already been referred to on p. 78.

COSTUME

(A) On brasses

DRUITT, Rev. Herbert. *A Manual of Costume as Illustrated in Monumental Brasses.* (De la More Press. 1906. 384 p. 110 illus.)

Useful for its illustrations, many of brasses actually *in situ*, but poor on armour and academic dress due to lack of understanding of the terminology, making it now of limited value. Short historical introduction on the development of brasses.

(B) General works

(Useful because they draw on brasses for examples, or for their concise descriptions of costume).

(1) PLANCHÉ, James R. *A Cyclopaedia of Costume . . .* 2 Vols. (1876–79. illus.)

This much quoted source draws heavily on brasses to illustrate the text and is still a standard work in the field. Unfortunately it is now only available in libraries or second-hand.

(2) KELLY, Francis M. and SCHWABE, Randolph. *A short history of Costume and Armour, chiefly in England, 1066–1800.* 2 Vols. (Batsford. 1931).

A useful reference source for those especially interested in armour, though not using many brasses as examples.

(3) CUNNINGTON, C. Willet and CUNNINGTON, Phyllis. *Handbook of Medieval English Costume.* (Faber. 36s. 0d. 1952. Repr. with corrections 1960. 192 p. illus.)

An excellent handbook for those wishing to give detailed descriptions of civilian costume as depicted on brasses. Armour and ecclesiastical vestments are not included. There is a good index, glossary and a short bibliography.

ARMOUR

(1) BLAIR, Claude. *European Armour.* (Batsford. 1958. 248 p. illus.)

A very thorough and useful work including many examples drawn from brasses, as well as photographs of actual suits of armour and many line drawings of the individual parts themselves. Regrettably now out of print.

(2) PUBLIC BUILDING AND WORKS, Ministry of. *An outline of Arms and Armour in England from the early Middle Ages to the Civil War*, by Sir James Mann. (H.M.S.O. 3s. 6d. 1960.)

An excellent handbook, well illustrated and including reproductions of a few brasses, one with the various parts of the armour labelled, i.e. Sir Hugh Hastings, Elsing, Norfolk. (1347); there is also a short list of works of reference.

(3) MANN, Sir James. *The Nomenclature of Armour.* M.B.S. Trans. Vol. 9. Pt. VIII. (Dec. 1961) pp. 414–428.

Illustrated with diagrams and quotations from contemporary documents; corrects many errors in earlier works on brasses e.g. Macklin.

ECCLESIASTICAL

See General list No. 14.

Major collections of brass rubbings

Most of the important collections are to be found in National Institutions, nearly all of them containing rubbings of great historical value, many of brasses since lost or mutilated. Amongst the largest the following may be mentioned:

(1) BRITISH MUSEUM (Dept. of MSS), Bloomsbury, London, W.C.1. Here one can see the famous historical collections of the pioneer brass rubbers, Craven Ord and Sir John Cullum (Add. MS. 32478) folded and tightly packed in wooden containers; the Francis Douce collection (Add. MS. 32479) rolled and mainly grouped by counties; that of the Rev. W. F. Creeny, and other miscellaneous collections, mainly of late nineteenth century date, e.g. Add. MS. 9064. These are mostly kept in large folders and usually available only on prior application, since they need special tables on which they can be inspected. There is an excellent article endeavouring to sort out the confusion over the Ord/Cullum/Douce collections, by the late V. J. Torr. in M.B.S. Trans. Vol. 9 (2). 1952. pp. 80–91 and Vol. 9 (3). 1954. pp. 133–145 entitled 'A Guide to Craven Ord'. Access to the British Museum Library and Department of Manuscripts is normally granted only to persons over 21 years of age; admission, once granted, is free; a reader's ticket must be produced at each visit, and must be renewed periodically.

(2) VICTORIA & ALBERT MUSEUM (Dept. of Engravings & Design), South Kensington, London, S.W.17. A large, and comprehensive, collection, arranged by type and then topographically. Permission to view the rubbings is best made in writing first – admission is free. The catalogue referred to earlier (p. 82) gives some idea of the scope of the collection. The Art Library and Print Room are

open daily (except Sundays and Public Holidays) from 10 a.m.

(3) SOCIETY OF ANTIQUARIES, Burlington House, Piccadilly, London, W.1. The most comprehensive of all the national collections, this too is arranged topographically and contains many rubbings made in the last century of great historical interest. Admission is granted to all serious students if application is made in writing to the Director, stating briefly your requirements and any other relevant details. The Society also has a large library containing many books, pamphlets, etc., on brasses and allied subjects and a complete set of the Monumental Brass Society Transactions. Access may also be given to the Library on prior application in writing as above.

(4) ASHMOLEAN MUSEUM (Library), Oxford. A good selection of rubbings, with special reference to the Oxford region. Arranged topographically. Admission by appointment only.

(5) BODLEIAN LIBRARY, Oxford. A selective, but valuable collection, containing many fine and important older rubbings. The library itself also holds collections of notes and drawings by early antiquaries like Richard Gough (ob. 1809), amongst which are a fine collection of drawings of lost French brasses made before the Revolution; Dr William Stukeley (ob. 1765) and Edward Steele; many references in these MS collections are to brasses, a large number since lost or defaced. The library is open to ticket holders only.

(6) UNIVERSITY MUSEUM OF ARCHAEOLOGY & ETHNOLOGY, Downing Street, Cambridge. Housed under the care of an Honorary Keeper, the collection is very nearly complete for the whole county, including the eighteenth century. Arranged topographically, the rubbings accepted must be

of a very high standard, and are kept in large portfolios. The Museum is open to the public on weekdays from 2–4 p.m. Application to view the rubbings must be made in writing and is only granted to serious students.

These are some of the largest British collections, but others of great interest and value will be found in other local Museums, Record Offices, and in some of the newer Universities (e.g. Pybus Collection, University Library, Newcastle-upon-Tyne.). Visits to some of these will be essential to anyone making special studies of individual regions or counties.

(7) MONUMENTAL BRASS SOCIETY (Founded 1887) Open to all interested in the study of brasses. One of the declared aims of the Society is 'to promote the study of, and interest in, monumental brasses, indents and incised slabs . . .' It also tries to ensure the proper protection and preservation of these memorials and hopes to compile a complete list of existing and lost British and Foreign brasses, indents and incised slabs (based on the lists of Mill Stephenson).

The annual subscription at the time of writing is £2 for full members, and £1 for associate members under 18 years of age. Both entitle one to receive one copy of the Transactions and Portfolio of the Society and to attend any meetings arranged. Membership at present is about 780 honorary, individual and institutional members. To all seriously interested in the study and protection of monumental brasses I strongly recommend your joining the Society. Full details of membership may be obtained from the Hon. Sec., 90 High Street, Newport Pagnell, Bucks. (or c/o The Society of Antiquaries, Burlington House, Piccadilly, London, W.1.).

APPENDIX

A short guide to the best brasses in the British Isles

The following list is intended only as a very general guide to those churches in the British Isles which, in the author's opinion, possess the most interesting brasses. No indication is given of the number at each church, and in several cases there is only one brass of special merit. While the list is not intended to be comprehensive, it does include most of the best brasses, not only for rubbing, but in the historical sense as well. Fees are now charged in most churches, and in some cases permission to rub the brasses may be given on certain days, e.g. Thame, Oxfordshire, or may even be refused except in very exceptional circumstances, e.g. Cobham, Kent. To be on the safe side it is always better to telephone or write first whenever possible.

Those churches marked with an asterisk (*) are those where the brasses are particularly fine, or of some special interest. For fuller details of those noted, and of other brasses, readers are referred to the lists of Mill Stephenson already quoted (p. 77). Continental brasses are not included as it is felt that any such list will be superseded by that compiled by Dr H. K. Cameron which is to be published shortly (see p. 78 for details). That given on page 110 of Malcolm Norris' book *Brass Rubbing* is the best checklist currently available.

BEDFORDSHIRE

Aspley Guise	Eyworth
Bedford (St Paul's)	Hatley Cockayne
*Bromham	Luton
Caddington	Marston Mortaine
*Cardington	*Shillington
Clifton	Sutton (plain cross)
*Cople	Turvey
Eaton Bray	*Wymington
*Elstow (abbess)	Yelden

106

BERKSHIRE

Appleton
Binfield
Blewbury
*Bray
*Childrey
Coxwell, Great
Denchworth (palimpsest)
Hanney, West
Marcham
Reading (St Laurence)

*Shottesbrooke
Sonning
Sparsholt
Stanford-in-the-Vale
Swallowfield
Wantage
*Windsor (St George's Chapel: rubbing not allowed except in special circumstances)
Wittenham, Little

BUCKINGHAMSHIRE

Chalfont St Giles
Chalfont St Peter
Chenies
Chicheley
Clifton Reynes (mutil.)
*Denham (abbess)
Dinton
*Drayton Beauchamp
*Edlesbororough
Ellesborough
*Eton College Chapel
Farnham Royal (interesting inscr.)
Halton (palimpsest)
Hampden, Great
Hedgerley (palimpsest)
Lillingstone Lovell
Middle Claydon
Nettleden

Over Winchendon
Penn
Pitstone
Quainton
Shalston
Slapton
Stokenchurch
Stoke Poges
Swanbourn
*Taplow
*Thornton
Tingewick
Twyford
*Tyringham
Waddesdon
Whaddon
Wooburn
Wooton Underwood
Wraysbury

CAMBRIDGESHIRE

**Balsham
*Burwell

Cambridge, Kings College
Cambridge, Trinity Hall

Cambridge, St Benedict's
Cambridge, St Mary-the-
  Less
Croxton
**Ely Cathedral
*Fulbourne
*Hildersham
Horseheath
Impington
*Isleham
Milton

Shelford, Little
Swaffham Priory (sev.
  examples from local
  workshop)
**Trumpington (1289; on
  tomb; covered with plate
  glass)
**Westley Waterless
Wilburton
Wimpole
Wisbech (worn)

Wood Ditton (part lost)

CHESHIRE

Chester. Holy Trinity
  (palimpsest)

*Macclesfield
Over

Wilmslow

CORNWALL

Blisland
Budock
Callington
Colan
Constantine
Illogan
Lanteglos-near-Fowey
Launeston (c. 1630,
  curious)

Mawgan-in-Pyder
Quethioc
St Columb Major
St Erme
St Just-in-Roseland
St Mellion
St Michael Penkivel
Stratton
Tintagel

CUMBERLAND

Carlisle Cathedral

Edenhall

DERBYSHIRE

Ashbourne
Dronfield
Edensor

Etwall
Hathersage
*Morley

Muggington
Norbury

Sawley
*Tideswell
Walton-on-Trent

DEVONSHIRE* †

*Dartmouth (St Saviour's)
*Exeter Cathedral
Haccombe (rubbing by
members of Mon. Br. Soc.
only)
Yealmpton

Harford
Petrockstow
Shillingford
*Stoke Fleming
Stoke-in-Teignhead

DORSET

Eversholt
Fleet (old church)
Milton Abbey
Piddletown

Thorncombe
*Wimborne Minster (royal
brass)
Yetminster

DURHAM

Haughton-le-Skerne

Houghton-le-Spring
Sedgefield

ESSEX

Arkesden
*Aveley
Bardfield, Great
Barking
Bowers Gifford (mutil.)
*Braxted, Little
Brightlingsea
Bromley, Great
*Chigwell (archbishop)
*Chrishall

Colchester. St Peter's
*Colchester Castle Museum
(brasses from Lit.
Horkesley)
Cressing
*Dagenham
*Easton, Little
Elmstead (curious)
Faulkbourne
Finchingfield

†For more detailed information see, Morris, *Mrs Q. Brass
Rubbing in Devon Churches*. (Available from the Author, Dartington
Rectory, Totnes, Devon. Price 5s. 9d. incl. postage. Published
1967).

*Gosfield
Halstead
Harlow (old church)
Hatfield Peverell (curious
  inscr. *c.* 1570)
Hempstead
*Horkesley, Little (see
  Colchester Castle
  Museum)
Ilford, Little
*Ingrave
Lambourne
Latton
Leigh-on-Sea
Littlebury
Nettleswell

North Ockendon
*Pebmarsh
Roydon
Runwell
Shelley (curious inscr.)
Stifford
Stock
Stondon Massey
Terling
Tilty
Tolleshunt Darcy (sev.
  palimpsest)
Upminster
Waltham Abbey
Wimbish (mutil.)
*Wivenhoe
Writtle

GLOUCESTERSHIRE

Bisley
Bristol. St John's
*Bristol. St Mary Redcliff
*Chipping Campden
*Cirencester
Clifford Chambers
*Deerhurst
Dyrham
*Fairford
Gloucs. St Mary-the Crypt

Leckhampton
Minchampton
Newland (mutil., curious
  crest)
*Northleach
Quinton
Rodmarton
Weston-upon-Avon
*Wormington (curious)
*Wooton-under-Edge

HAMPSHIRE

Brown Candover
*Crondall
Eversley (cross; curious)
*Havant
Headbourne Worthy
  (schoolboy)

Kimpton
Kings Sombourne
Odiham
Sherborne St John
Southwick
Stoke Charity

*Thruxton
Warnborough, South
Whitchurch

Winchester. College
   Chapel & Cloisters
*Winchester. St Cross

HEREFORDSHIRE

Clehonger
*Hereford Cathedral
Ledbury

Ludford
Marden (lady, curious
   hairstyle, 1614)

HERTFORDSHIRE

*Aldbury
Aldenham
Aspenden
Baldock (mutil.)
*Berkhamsted, Great
  (mural on boards; some
  difficult to reach)
*Broxbourne
Buckland
*Clothall
*Digswell
Essendon (high on wall)
Flamstead (worn)
*Furneaux Pelham
*Hemel Hempstead
*Hinxworth
Hitchin
Hunsdon (curious 'death's signe' brass)

Kings Langley
*Knebworth (damaged
  1968)
*Hadham, Much (or Great)
*Mimms, North
Radwell
**At Alban's Abbey (Dela-
  mare br. not for rubbing
  because of damage)
*St Albans. St Michael's
*Sawbridgeworth
*Standon
Walkern
Watford (mutil.)
*Watton-at-Stone
Wormley
Wyddial

HUNTINGDONSHIRE

Diddington (mutil.)
Offard D'Arcy

Sawtry. All Saints
Stilton

ISLE OF WIGHT

Calbourne
Freshwater

Kingston
Shorwell

KENT

Addington
Ash-next-Sandwich
Ashford (mutil.)
Aylesford
*Beckenham
Bexley (unusual)
Biddenham
Birchington
Bobbing (Speaker of
    House of Commons,
    1410; mutil.)
Boughton-under-Blean
Brabourne
Canterbury. St George's
Canterbury. St Martin's
Chart, Great
*Chartham
***Cobham (v. fine series;
    rubbing not permitted)
*Dartford
Eastry
Erith
*Faversham
*Graveney
Halling, Lower
*Hardres, Upper
Headcorn
*Herne
**Hever
Hoo St Werburgh

*Horsmonden
Horton Kirby
Kemsing
Lullingstone
*Lydd
*Maidstone. All Saints
Malling, East
*Margate
Mereworth
Milton-next-Sittingbourne
**Minster, Isle of Sheppey
*Northfleet
Otterden
Pluckley (sev. restored)
Preston-next-Faversham
St Mary Cray (last
    English brasses, but not
    suitable for rubbing)
Saltwood
Seal
Sheldwich
Southfleet
*Stone
Sutton, East
Ulcombe
Upchurch
Westerham
Wickham, East
Wickham, West
*Woodchurch

Wrotham

LANCASHIRE

Childwall
Eccleston
*Manchester Cathedral
Middleton

Ormskirk
Preston
Sefton
Whalley

Winwick

Plate 15.
Reproduced from
Portfolio Mon.
Brass Soc. Vol. I Part
VI, pl. 6. Indent of
brass of Bishop
Beaumont (*ob.* 1333).
Durham Cathedral.
Bishop Beaumont's
brass is the largest
example known, and
although none of the
original remains, the
figure was restored in
1951. The whole slab,
of which the above is a
late nineteenth century
copy, measures some
15 ft high by 10 ft
wide. (*See Chapter 1.*)
*By courtesy of the
Monumental Brass Soc.*

Plate 16. *Left* St Alban. *Right* King Offa. These two figures are photographic enlargements from the negative of Plate 4. The prints have been cut to shape and mounted on a black background to make unusual bookmarks. (*See Chapter 4.*)

LEICESTERSHIRE

*Bottesford
Castle Donington
Launde
Sheepshed
Stapleford

Sibstone (also spelt
  Sibson)
Stockerston
Thurcaston (mutil.)
Wanlip

LINCOLNSHIRE

Althorpe
Barton-on-Humber. St
  Mary's
Bigby
*Boston (worn; some fine
  incised slabs)
*Broughton
*Buslingthorpe (half eff.,
  c. 1310)
*Croft (half eff., c. 1300)
Edenham (curious)
Evedon
Gedney (mutil.)
Grainthorpe
Gunby
Hainton

Harrington
Horncastle
Ingoldmells
Irnham
Kelsey, South
Laughton
*Linwood
Norton Disney
  (palimpsest)
Ormsby, South
Scrivelsby (local; curious)
*Spilsby
*Stamford. All Saints
**Tattershall
Theddlethorpe All Saints
Wrangle

LONDON (City & Westminster)

*All Hallows, Barking   St Helen's, Bishopsgate
*Westminster Abbey (Rubbing stopped 1968)

LONDON (Greater London incl. former County of Middlesex)

Chelsea
Ealing
*Enfield
Finchley
*Fulham (Flemish brass)
Greenford, Great

Hackney
Harlington
**Harrow
Hayes
*Hillingdon
Ickenham

Isleworth (damaged by
fire)
Islington. St Mary's

Monken Hadley
Northolt
West Drayton (palimp.)

Willesden

MONMOUTH
Matherne

NORFOLK

Aldborough
Aylsham (curious;
shrouded skeletons)
Bawburgh
Beechamwell
*Blickling
Buckenham, Old (curious)
*Burnham Thorpe
Cley
Creake, North
Ditchingham
**Elsing (in locked recess
let into chancel floor)
Erpingham
**Felbrigg
Fransham, Great
Frenze
Halvergate (palimpsest)
Helhoughton (curious;
part lost)
Hellesdon
Holme-next-the-Sea
**Hunstanton. Old Church
(on high tomb)
Ketteringham

**Kings Lynn. St
Margaret's (two fine
Flemish brasses)
Merton
Methold (damaged)
Mulbarton (curious)
Narborough
*Necton
Newton Flotman
Norwich. St George's
Colgate
**Norwich. St John
Maddermarket
Norwich. St Lawrence
Norwich. St Peter Hun-
gate Museum
Norwich. St Stephen's
Ormesby, Great
Paston
Reedham (curious)
Rougham
*Sherbourne
*South Acre
Upwell
Wiveton (curious)

Worsted

NORTHAMPTONSHIRE

Ashby St Ledgers
Ashton

Blakesley
Blisworth

Brampton-by-Dingley
*Castle Ashby
Charwelton
*Cotterstock (bracket
  brass)
Dene
Dodford
Easton Neston
Fawsley
Greens Norton
Heythrop
**Higham Ferrers

*Lowick
Marholm
*Newton-by-Geddington
*Rothwell
Somerton
Sudborough
Sulgrave (ancestors of
  George Washington,
  U.S. President; mutil.)
Wappenham (some
  mutil.)
Warkworth
Welford

NORTHUMBERLAND

*Newcastle-upon-Tyne. All Saints. (covered by glass)

NOTTINGHAMSHIRE

Clifton
Hickling
Markham, East

*Newark (Flemish)
Strelley
Wellaton

OXFORDSHIRE

Adderbury
Bampton
*Brightwell Baldwin
Broughton
Burford
Cassington (cross)
Charlton-on-Otmoor
Checkendon
*Chinnor
Chipping Norton (some
  mutil.)
*Dorchester
*Ewelme (rubbing certain
  days only)

Haseley, Great
Mapledurham (private
  chapel; no rubbing at
  present)
Oxford. Christchurch
  Cathedral
Oxford. Magdalen
  College
*Oxford. Merton College
**Oxford. New College
*Oxford. Queen's College
Oxford. St John's College
Oxford. St Aldgate's
  Church

Oxford. St Cross Church,
  Holywell
Oxford. St Michael
  (Northgate)
Rotherfield Greys
Shipton-under-Wychwood
  (palimpsest)
Somerton
Stanton Harcourt
Stoke Lyne

Newnham Murren
  (damaged by musket ball)
*Noke
Nuffield
Oddington (curious)
Tew, Great
*Thame (rubbing Mon.,
  Tues., Wed. only)
*Waterperry
Whitchurch
Witney

RUTLAND
*Little Casterton

SHROPSHIRE

*Acton Burnell
Adderley
Edgemond

Ightfield
*Tong
Upton Cressett

SOMERSET

Banwell
Beckington
Burnett
Hutton
*Ilminster
Luccombe

Petherton, South
*St Decumans
Shepton Mallet (curious)
Swainswick
Wedmore
Yeovil

STAFFORDSHIRE

Audley
Clifton Campville (mutil.)
Horton
Kinver

Norbury
*Okeover (palimpsest)
Standon (sm. cross)
Trentham

SUFFOLK

**Acton (v. fine military
  br., ? 1302)

Aldeburgh
Barrow

Barsham
Bradley, Little
Brundish
*Burgate
Depden
Easton
*Gorleston (*c.* 1320;
  mutil.)
Hawstead
Ipswich. Christ Church
  Mansion Museum (br.
  of Thos. Poynder from
  bombed church of St
  Mary Quay)
Ipswich. St Mary Tower

Ixworth
Lavenham
*Letheringham
Mendham
Mendlesham (part lost)
Orford
*Playford
Ringsfield (tomb outside
  church)
*Rougham
Sotterley
**Stoke-by-Nayland
Wenham, Little
Wrentham
*Yoxford

SURREY

Addington
*Beddington
Betchworth
Bletchingley
Bookham, Great
Byfleet (under glass)
Camberwell. St Giles'
Carshalton (some
  mutil.)
Cheam
Clapham. St Peter's
Cobham (under glass)
Cranley (curious)
Crowhurst
Ewell
Horley

*Horsley, East
*Lingfield
Mickleham
Oakwood (under glass)
Ockham
Peper-Harow
Richmond
Shere
***Stoke d'Abernon (1277;
  oldest figure br. in U.K.;
  rubbing by prior booking
  only)
*Thames Ditton
Thorpe
*Walton-on-Thames
  (curious)

SUSSEX

*Amberley
Ardingly

*Arundel
Battle

Broadwater
Burton
Buxted
*Clapham
**Cowfold (v. fine monastic br.)
Etchingham
Fletching
Grinstead, East
Grinstead, West

*Horsham
Hurstmonceaux
Ore (mutil.)
Pulborough
Slaugham
Stopham (sev. restored)
**Trotton
Warbleton
Warminghurst
West Firle
Wiston

WARWICKSHIRE

Baginton
Coleshill
Compton Verney
Coughton
Haseley (palimpsest)
Merevale

Middleton
*Warwick. St Mary's (difficult to rub; high on wall)
Wellesbourne-Hastings
*Wixford

WESTMORLAND

Kendal
Musgrave, Great (part lost)

WILTSHIRE

Alton Priors (curious)
Berwick Basset
Bradford-on-Avon
Bromham
*Cliffe Pypard
*Dauntsey

*Draycot Cerne
*Fovant
Lacock
Mere
**Salisbury Cathedral
Tisbury
Wanborough

WORCESTERSHIRE

Daylesford
Fladbury

*Strensham
Tredington
*Kidderminster (fine but worn)

YORKSHIRE

(N.R.=North Riding; E.R.=East Riding; W.R.= West Riding)

*Aldborough (near Boroughbridge W.R.)
Allerton (W.R.)
Beeford (E.R.)
Bolton-by-Bowland (W.R.)
*Brandsburton (E.R.)
*Cottingham (E.R. mutil.)
*Cowthorpe (W.R.)
*Harpham (E.R.)

Owston (W.R.)
Rawmarsh (W.R.)
Routh (E.R. mutil.)
Sessay (N.R.)
Skipton-in-Craven (W.R.)
Sprotborough (W.R.)
*Topcliffe (N.R.)
**Wensley (N.R.)
York Minster (mutil. Rubbing stopped 1968)

SCOTLAND

*Aberdeen. St Nicholas'
Glasgow Cathedral

Edinburgh. St Giles' (palimpsest)

WALES

Beaumaris (Anglesey)
Bettws Cedewen (Montgomery)
Llanbeblig (Caernarvon)
Whitchurch (Denbigh)

Llanrwst (Denbigh; interesting 17th cent. series)
Ruthin (Denbigh)
Swansea (Glamorgan)

IRELAND
see pp. 99–100

BRASSES IN MUSEUMS, SOCIETIES, ETC.

Over the years a good many brasses, or parts of brasses, have found their way into Museums, largely as a result of the two World Wars; others have come from derelict churches, auctions, 'junk' shops and similar sources. In the United Kingdom by far the largest number can be seen in the British Museum and the Victoria and Albert Museum in London. Many provincial Museums also possess examples, e.g. Saffron Walden, Essex; St Peter Hungate and Norwich Castle Museums, Norwich, Norfolk. Apart from an unknown number in private possession, several Archaeological Societies hold examples, a very large number being held by the Society of Antiquaries of London. Many of the brasses on the Continent are now housed in Museums as a direct result of the two World Wars.

INDEX

Note: This index includes all subjects, proper names and authors and titles of books/periodical articles referred to in Chapters 1–4. For Chapter 5 and Appendix I respectively, author's surnames and Counties or Countries only are indexed. Where the author is a corporate body, e.g. Ashmolean Museum, this is indexed accordingly.

The letter (L) after a page number indicates a reference to the list of best brasses given in Appendix I (pp. 106–119).

Similarly, the letter (B) refers to the list of books/articles about that area or place in Chapter 5 (pp. 76–102).

A small letter (n) indicates a footnote on the page cited.

Any page numbers in parentheses indicates a passing reference only to the subject/author.

Aberdeen, St Nicholas' Church, 20, 99(B)
Academical brasses, classification, 72
Acton (Suffolk), 65, 74
Addington, Rev. H., 87(B)
Aitcheson, L., *History of metals*, 16
Aldenham (Herts.), abuse of brasses, 23
Aluminium Federation, 54
Amwell, Great (Herts.), brasses stolen, 24
Ancient brass engraving, 29
Andrews, H. C., 91(B)
W. F., 91(B)
Antiquaries, Society of, 104, (120)
Appropriated brasses, 24
Arabia, Lawrence of, brass, rubbings, 23
Armour, books on, 102
Ashmolean Museum, 78 (B) 84–5(B), 104

Badger, Rev. E. W., 97–8(B)
Barnard, E. A. B., 98(B)
Beauchamp, Simon de, 13
Beaumont, E. T., 82(B)
Beaumont, Bishop L. von, 19, *Pl.* 15
Beauty in Brass, 29
Beckington (Somerset), *Pl.* 12
Bedford, St Paul's Church, 13,
Bedfordshire, (21), 87(B) 106(L)
Belcher, W. D., 92(B)
Beloe, E. M., 93(B), 94(B)
Belonje, Dr J., 100(B)
Berkhamsted, Gt (Herts.), 15 (45)
Berkshire, 87(B), 107 (L)
Blair, C., 102(B)
Bouquet, Rev. A. C., 78(B), 83–4(B), 86(B), (100)
Boutell, Rev. C., 79(B)
Bower, Canon R., 89(B)
Brass
    analysis of, 16

Brass *(continued)*—
  composition of metal, 15–16
  enamelling, 18
  engraving, method, 17
  engraving, schools of, 18
  largest English, 19
  manufacture of, 14, 16
  oldest, known, 13; surviv-
    ing, 14, 117(L)
Brasses
  best in U.K., 106–19
  care of when rubbing, 46
  classification by type, 71–3
  colour used on, 18
  comparative sizes of, 19, 20
  Continental
    books about, 100–1
    classification, (72)
    history, 13–19
    rubbing, 38–9, *Pls.* 4, 14
  cost, 20–1
  design, 17–19
  destruction, 21–3
  distribution, 21
  engraving, method, 17
  facsimiles, 66–7
  fixing in slab, method, 18
  Flemish, *see* Brasses, Con-
    tinental
  guide to best in U.K., 106–
    20
  in private possession, 119–
    20
  manufacture, 14
  mis-use of, 23
  numbers of, 13
  origin, 13–15
  palimpsest, 24–5
  recording, for historical pur-
    poses, 74
  special types, e.g. shroud,
    72–3

Brasses *(continued)*—
  theft of, 22–4
  unrecorded, notification of,
    21
Brass rubbing
  abroad, 38–9
  aluminium foil, use of, 53–4,
    Pls. 10, 11
  alternative methods, 47–54
  at the universities, 38
  bookcloth, 49(n)
  history, 25–8
  mural brasses, problems, 45
  materials required, choice
    of, 31–7, 47–50
  method, 39–54
  new materials (e.g. colours),
    47–50.
  note-taking for record pur-
    poses, 44
  'reverse' method, 50–1, *Pl.* 9
  traditional methods, 39–43
Brass Rubbing, see Norris,
  Malcolm
Brass rubbings
  cataloguing, 70–5
  charges for making, 37
  display, 55–8
  exhibitions, public, 64–6
  indexing, 73–5
  mounting, 56–8
  national collections in U.K.,
    103–5
  photographing, 58–60
  storage, methods, 68–70
*Brief notes concerning Monu-
  mental Brasses on the Continent . . .* , 39
Briscoe, J. P., 95(B)
Bristol, (18)
British Museum, 96(B), 103,
  (119)

Bromham (Beds.), palimpsest, 24
Broxbourne (Herts.), 18
Bruges, (19)
Buckinghamshire, (21), 107 (L)
Building in England down to 1540, 17
Bülow, Henry von, 19
Ludolph, 19
Bures, Sir Robert de, 65, 74
Busby, R. J., 91(B)
Bushnell, G. S., 94(B)
Butterworth, L. M. A., 89(B)

Cambridge, (18)
City Libraries, 88(B)
University, 38
Association of Brass Collectors, 80(B)
Monumental Brass Society, 90(B)
Cambridgeshire, 88(B), 107–8(L)
Camera Copying and Reproduction, 60
Cameron, Dr H. K., (78) (93(B), (101), (106)
(and Norris, M. W.), *Brief notes concerning Monumental Brasses on the Continent of Europe*, 39
Metals used in Monumental Brasses, 29
Care of brasses, when rubbing, 46
Casmiri, Cardinal Frederick, 19
Cataloguing brass rubbings, 70–5
Catling, H. W., 78(B)
Cave, C. J. P., 88, 91(B)

Chancellor, F., 90(B)
Charlton, O. J., 88(B)
Cheshire, 88–9(B), 108(L)
Christy, M., 90(B)
Chinnor (Oxon.), 19
Civilian brasses, classification, 72
Clayton, Rev. H. J., 83
Cobham (Kent), 38, (106)
Colby (Norfolk), palimpsest, 25
Collections, national, of brass rubbings, 103–5
Cologne, 16, (18)
Colour of Heraldry, 49
Connor, A. B., 96(B)
Continental brasses, *see* Brasses, Continental
Cook, Malcolm, 78, 85(B)
Cornwall, 89(B), 108(L)
Costume, books on, 101–2
Cotman, J. S., 94(B), 96(B)
Coventry, (18)
Crabbe, W. R., 89(B)
Cracow, (18), 19
Crayons, use of, for rubbings, 47–9
Creeny, Rev. W. F., (86), 100, (103)
Creke, Sir John, 17
Croy, O. R., *Camera Copying and Reproduction*, 60
Cullen plates, 16
Cullum, Sir John, 26, 103
Cumberland, (21), 89(B), 108(L)
Cunnington, C. W., 102
Phyllis, 102
Dabbings, early example, 28
making, 51–2
D'Abernon, Sir John, 18
Stoke, Church, (38), 117

Davis, Cecil T., 90, 91, 98, 99 (all (B))
Davy, David E., 96
De Beauchamp, *see* Beauchamp
De Bures, *see* Bures
De la Mare, Abbot Thomas, of St Albans, (19), *Pl. 4*
D'Elboux, R. H., 97(B)
Derbyshire, 89(B), 108–9(L)
Detail paper, 33–4, 49
Devonshire, 89(B), 109(L)
Digswell (Herts.), 65–6, *Pls. 1, 8*
palimpsest at, 24–5
Dorset, 89–90(B), 109(L)
Douce, Francis, 26, (103)
Dowsing, William, 22–3
Druitt, Rev. H., 101(B)
Dublin, 99–100(B)
Dunkin, E. H. W., 89(B)
Durer, woodcut, copied for brass, 19
Durham Cathedral, 19, *Pl. 15*
County, (21), 95(B), 109 (L)

Ecclesiastical brasses, classification, 72
Edinburgh, St Giles' Church, 99(B)
Edlesborough (Bucks.), palimpsest, 25
Eire, *see* Ireland
English Monumental Brass Rubbings, 29
English Monumental Brasses of the 15th and Early 16th centuries, 29
Engraving, *see* Brass, engraving
Essex, (21), 90(B), 109–10 (L)

Evans, Major H. F. Owen, 71, (100)
Evelyn, John, at Lincoln, 22
Exhibitions, of brass rubbings, 64–6
catalogue, making of, 65–6

Facsimiles of brasses, 66–7
Fairbank, F. R., 99(B)
Farrer, Rev. E., 94(B), 96(B)
Felbrigg, Sir John, 23
Field, Rev. H. E., 67, 89(B), 95(B)
Fisher, Thomas, drawings, 27, 87(B), 92(B)
Flemish brasses, *see* Brasses, Continental
Folcard, Rev. Richard, brass, *Pl. 9*
Franklyn, J., 84(B)
Freiberg, (17)
French, Rev. V., 92(B)

Gadd, M. L., *English Monumental Brasses of the 15th and Early 16th centuries*, 29
Gawthorp, W. E., *Ancient brass engraving*, 29
Brasses . . . , 89(B)
Ghent, (18)
Gloucestershire, 90(B), 110 (L)
Glues, *see* Paste
Gothic World, 1100–1600, 29
Gough, R., *Sepulchral Monuments . . .* , 26
Greenhill, F. A., *Incised Slabs of Leicestershire and Rutland*, 29
other works, 94(B), 99(B), 100(B)

Griffin, R., 92(B), 93(B)
Gunther, R. T., 95(B)

Haines, Rev. H., (18), 77(B), 80(B), 91(B)
Halyburton, Andrew, ledger, 20
Hamburg, (18)
Hampshire, 91(B), 110–11(L)
Hampton-Poyle (Oxon.), *Pl.* 11
Harrow (Middx), palimpsest, 24
Hartsthorne, Rev. C. H., 94 (B)
Harvey, John, *Gothic World* . . . , 29
Heel-ball, choice of for rubbing, black, 34–5
coloured, 47
composition, 27, 34
first made, 27
Heraldry Society, *Colour of Heraldry*, 49
Herefordshire, 91(B), 111(L)
Hermanszoen, Arnout, contract for brass, 16
Hertfordshire, (21), 91(B), 111(L)
Hilliger, family, 17
Hinxworth (Herts.), 45
History of Metals, 16
Houston, C. E. D. D., 97(B)
Hudson, F., 94(B)
Humberstone, Annas, *Pl.* 2; Edward, *Pl.* 2
Humfre, Thomas, goldsmith, brass, 15
Huntingdonshire, 92(B), 111 (L)

Illsley, S. A., 66

Incised slabs, 14
Incised Slabs of Leicestershire and Rutland, 29
Indents, recording, 25, 52–3
Indexing brass rubbings, 73–5
Ingram, A. J. W., 91(B)
Introducing Screen Printing, 61
Ipswich, (18)
Ireland, (21), 99–100(B)
Isherwood, G. and K., 87(B)
Isle of Wight, 92(B), 111(L)

Jeans, Rev. G. E., 93(B)
Jenkins, C. K., *Beauty in Brass*, 29
Jones, Wm. B., *English Monumental Brass Rubbings*, 29

Kelly, F. M., 101(B)
Kelshall (Herts.), 23
Kent, (21), 92–3(B), 112(L)
Kent, Dr J. P. C., *Monumental brasses; a new Classification of Military Effigies*, 73
Kinsey, A., *Introducing Screen Printing*, 61
Simple Screen Printing, 61
Kite, E., 98(B)

Lancashire, 88(B), 112(L)
Laton, 16
Latten, 16
Laurent Designs Ltd, 66–7, *Pl.* 13
Lawrence, T. E., brass rubbings, 28
Leicestershire, 113(L)
Lewis, R. M. W., 92(B)
Liddel, Dr Duncan, brass, 20
Liége, (18)
Limoges, enamels, 18
Lincoln, Cathedral, 22, 93(B)

Lincolnshire, 93(B), 113(L)

Lining paper, for rubbings, 31–2

Llanwrest (Denbigh), 99(B)

London, City of, & Westminster, 93(B), 113(L)

School of engraving, (18)

Lübek, (18)

Macalister, R. A. S., 88(B)

Macklin, Rev. H. W., 77, 81–2, 92, 97, 99 (all (B))

Mann, Sir James, 73, 84(B), 86(B), 102(B)

Manning, C. R., 76(B)

Masefield, C., 96(B)

Mason, Walter the, 17

Matrix, *see* Indents

M.B.S. Transactions, *see Monumental Brass Society Transactions*

Mediaeval Trade in Monumental Brasses, 29

Meissen, (18)

Meopham (Kent), 23

Metals used in Monumental Brasses, 29

Middlesex, 93(B), 113–4(L)

Military brasses, classification, 71, 73

Mimms, North (Herts.), 19

Misselbrook, C. G., 93

Monmouthshire, 114(L)

Monumental Brass Society, 21, 25, 38, 53, 81(B), 92(B), 105

Portfolio, 81, 105

Transactions, 24, 81, 105

Monumental Brasses; a new classification of Military Effigies, 29

Morley, H. T., 87(B)

Morris, Mrs Q., *Brass rubbing in Devon Churches*, 109(n)

Mosse, H. R., 97(B)

Mural brasses, rubbing, problems of, 45

National collections of brass rubbings, 103–105

Neale, J. M., 88(B)

Newcastle-upon-Tyne,

All Saints' Church, *Pl.* 14

University Library, 105

Norfolk, (21), 94(B), 114(L)

Norris, Malcolm W.

Brass Rubbing, 17, 29, 71, (78), 85(B), (101), 106

Mediaeval Trade in Monumental Brasses, 29

Schools of Brasses in Germany, 19, 30, 101

(and Cameron, H. K.) *Brief Notes Concerning Monumental Brasses on the Continent of Europe*, 39

Northamptonshire, 94(B), 114–15(L)

Northumberland, (21), 95(B), 115(L)

Norwich, (18)

Castle Museum, 120

St Peter Hungate Museum, 119

Notes, making of when rubbing, 43–4; *see also* Indexing

Nottinghamshire, 95(B), 115 (L)

Nürnberg, 17, (18)

Okeover (Staffs.), palimpsest, 25

Ord, Craven, 26, 103

Ormiston (E. Lothian), 99(B)

Oxford
  Journal of Monumental Brasses, 81
  Portfolio of Monumental Brasses, 81
  University
    Archaeological Society, 81, 95
    Architectural Society, 79–80
    Brass rubbing at, 38
    Brass Rubbing Society, 81
Oxfordshire, 95(B), 115–6(L)

Packington (Leics.), brass stolen, 24
Page-Phillips, J. C., 49(n), 77(n)
Pakefield (Suffolk), *Pl.* 9
Palimpsest brasses, 24–5, (78), (84), *Pl.* 2, 3
Pantograph, for copying rubbings, 67–8
Paper
  choice of for brass rubbing, 31–3, 49–50
  fixing when rubbing, 36, 41, 45
Paris, (18)
Parker, Elizabeth, *Pl.* 7
  J. F., 98(B)
Paste, for mounting rubbings, 57–8
Pearson, R. H., (100)
Peryent, Sir John (snr), 65, *Pl.* 1
  Sir John (jnr), *Pl.* 8
Phillips & Page Ltd, 33
  (address), 49
Photographing brass rubbings, 58–60
Planché, J. R., 101(B)

Playford (Suffolk), 23
Porteous, W.W., 90(B)
Poyle, Elizabeth, *Pl.* 11
  Sir John, *Pl.* 11
Prideaux, W. de C., 89(B)
Pybus Collection of brass rubbings, 105

Radwell (Herts.), *Pl.* 7
Reed, Dr Thomas, 53
Regensburg, oldest surviving brass, 14
Renaud, F., 100(B)
Richardson, H. S., heel-ball, 27
Rogers, W. H. H., 89(B)
Royston (Herts.), brass used as door-scraper, 23
Ruck, G. A. E., 94(B)
Royal Commission on Historical Monuments, 88(B), 93(B), 95(B)
Rutland, 116(L)

Saffron Walden Museum (Essex), 119
St Albans Abbey (Herts.), 19, *Pl.* 4
Salzman, L. F. *Building in England down to 1540*, 17
Sanderson, H. K. St J., 87(B)
Sandys, Sir William, contract for brass, 16
Say, Sir John, 18
Schelewaerts, Jacob, brass, 19
Schools of Brasses in Germany, 19, 30, 101
Schwabe, R., 101(B)
Scotland, (21), 99(B), 114(L)
Screen printing, from rubbings, 60–4, *Pl.* 12
Sepulchral Monuments of G.B., 26

Seyntmour, Elizabeth, *Pl.* 12
Sir John, *Pl.* 12
Shrewsbury, St Alkmund's Church, 23
Shropshire, 95(B), 116(L)
Simple screen printing, 61
Simpson, J., 77(B)
Society of Antiquaries of London, *see* Antiquaries, Society of
Somerset, 96(B), 116(L)
Staffordshire, 96(B), 116(L)
Stephenson, Mill, 77–8(B), 95(B), 96(B), 99(B)
Stone, P. G., 92(B)
Storage, of brass rubbings, 67–70
Street, Dr William, 53
Suffling, E. R., 82(B)
Suffolk, (21), 96(B), 116–17(L)
Surrey, 96–7(B), 117(L)
Sussex, 97(B), 117–8(L)

Thacker, F. J., 98(B)
Thame (Oxon.), 106
Thornley, J. L., 88(B)
Thornton, Roger, brass, *Pl.* 14
Society, 95(B)
Torr, V. J., 103(B)
Trivick, H., 86(B)
Trumpington (Cambs.), (38), 108(L)

Universities, brass rubbing at, 38; (*see also* under place names)
University Museum of Archaeology and Ethnology, Cambridge, 104–5

Victoria & Albert Museum, 82–3(B), 103–4, (119)
Vischer, family, (17)
Von Bülow, *see* Bülow

Wales, (21), 99(B), 119(L)
Walkern (Herts.), palimpsest, (24), *Pls.* 2, 3
Waller, J. G., 80(B), 95(B)
L. A. B., 80(B)
Walton-on-Thames (Surrey), palimpsest, 25
Ward, J. S. M., 82(B)
Warwickshire, 97–8(B), 118 (L)
Wasters, 25
Way, Albert, *Sepulchral Brasses, and Incised Slabs*, 30, 32
Westley Waterless (Cambs.), 17
Westminster
Abbey, 93(B), 113(L)
St Margaret's Church, 22
Westmorland, 89(B), 118(L)
Williams, Charles, 97(B)
Wiltshire, 98(B), 118(L)
Windsor & Newton Ltd, paper, 33, 49
Woodman, T. C., 97(B)
Worcestershire, 98(B), 118 (L)
Workshops, brass, 16–18
Wyisman, Alexander, 20

Yevele, Henry, mason, 14
York, (18)
Minster, weather vane, of brass, 23
Yorkshire, 99(B), 119(L)